to Ruth

Best wishes.

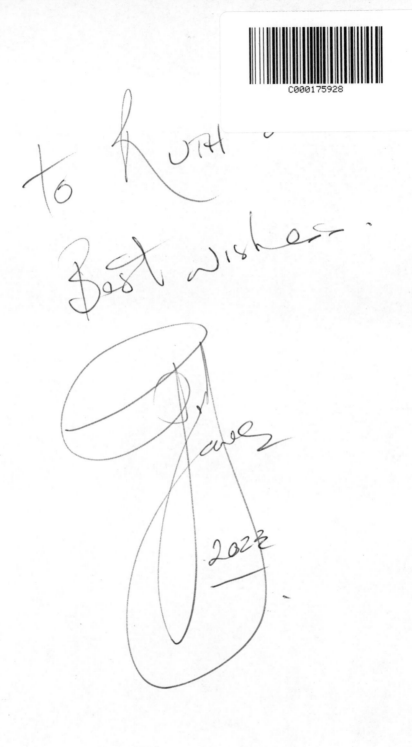

2022

AMAZED

GEORGE
JONES

Dedication

Without any doubt I have been blessed with the most amazing family who have been a constant support. My dear sister and queen, Lally, has been like a second mother and has always been there for me. I have a wonderful son, Jason, a beautiful daughter, Natalie, and three precious grandchildren, who I wouldn't be without. But the one person who has stayed by my side, unselfishly, and supported and loved me unconditionally, is my very special and incredible wife, my first lady Hilary. Finally, I would like to acknowledge my Lord, who has blessed me abundantly.

AMAZED

Copyright © 2022 by George Jones

ISBN: 978-1-915223-15-9

Published by

Maurice Wylie Media

Your Inspirational & Christian Publisher

For more information visit

www.MauriceWylieMedia.com

Endorsements

I have known George for many years and have enjoyed numerous chats on his radio shows. He has always been there for me when I needed help with publicity for worthy causes. We also worked together closely on the Duke of Edinburgh Award and the President's Award during the Troubles in Northern Ireland, to make both awards available for the young people of Northern Ireland.

Over the years I have become firm friends with George and his dear wife Hilary.

I wish him every success with his book.

Dame Mary Peters, LG, CH, DBE, Lady Companion of the Order of the Garter.

Having known George Jones since we both were kids; I can't wait to get into these pages; this is the unique story about one of Ireland's star entertainers with a great life and an amazing message about how it all came to be. Expect this book to encourage you.

Leslie Holmes, Ph.D., D.Min.

I can still see my late father sitting in our family caravan in Portrush, tears streaming down his face that was alight with laughter as we sat around the table listening to a cassette tape he had just bought entitled, *Clubsound Capers*. The tracks from that recording such as, *Tonga LOL* and *Shankill Airways* are fondly remembered by so many of us, who recall life in the days before mobile phones, online streaming and music downloads. This old cassette tape was my first exposure to Clubsound and probably dates back to the summer of 1980. Little did I know then, as a young boy, that I would someday have the privilege of writing this forward to George Jones' autobiography.

I first met George in 1992, when he was presenting his radio programme, *Just Jones* on BBC Radio Ulster. George had invited my band, Live Issue, onto his programme to talk about our music and to perform a couple of songs live in the studio.

With the benefit of hindsight, it is very apparent how George Jones and Clubsound played an important role in sustaining the emotional wellbeing of so many people in Northern Ireland during the dark days of the Troubles.

Through the medium of radio, George followed on from what Clubsound had been doing in their stage shows during the 1990s and early 2000s. His *Just Jones* show became, by far, the most popular programme on local radio. As in previous years, George used his radio programme as a vehicle for laughter and entertainment. In addition, he helped his audience come to terms with traumatic events both locally and worldwide, including the Omagh Bomb and 9/11. He also gave people a forum to openly share their thoughts and feelings during these intense times of grief and confusion.

George is now playing bass guitar in a Christian band called, Heart and Soul. The band's name is the same as the television programme he presented twenty years ago; however, now that George has given his life to the Lord, he can really sing those songs of faith and redemption from a personal perspective and from his own heart and soul.

I hope you enjoy George's story of music, laughter and faith.

Colin Elliott, Secretary to the Gospel Music Association Northern Ireland and Fellow Musicianary.

Contents

Foreword 1

Some people would say that George and I are chalk and cheese, but it turns out that those two ingredients in a producer and a presenter make a really good mix for live radio. Blend them together and bake in a musical microwave, to make a top-rated programme and its less chalk and cheese, more cheese and crackers.

You can't overestimate the love from listeners for a daily radio show, especially during the worst of times, but it needs to be something to lift the spirits and give you a laugh as well.

The trick that George has mastered, is to combine his light-hearted banter from a lifetime in the entertainment business with a capacity to tackle the most heart-rending tragedy. George took it all on in the years we worked together.

It was a programme that took us across the world, but some of its most poignant moments were the homegrown grass-roots ones here in Northern Ireland.

George can handle whatever a producer throws at him, but even he was momentarily taken aback one Valentine's Day. We'd asked what love is and we were getting the usual bouquets of roses and cups of tea in bed.

Suddenly a woman caller said, 'Love is taking a bullet for your partner.' It still sends a shiver down my spine. George looked through the production desk glass at me and I indicated that he should continue the conversation. It was a woman whose family had been in a gospel hall, when terrorist gunmen raked elders with bullets and proceeded into the County Armagh church. His caller told the tale.

It was the only occasion that George coped with the tragedy of terrorism. We all wept when we met the brave firefighters in New York who had lived through the trauma of 9/11. At home, he fielded call after call about the shocking massacre of innocents from the Omagh bomb.

A lot of our work was about fun, of course, whether it was the multi million-pound fundraising from George's auction for *Children in Need,* or the young entertainers assembled for the annual Christmas concert in the Ulster Hall.

Ulster's finest youngsters were on-air every afternoon. The door was also open for the young wheelchair user who often came on the show to talk about her resilient approach to life. Michaela, is now a global campaigner on issues to do with differently abled young people. From such little acorns, grow big strong oaks.

I haven't mentioned the countless celebrities — world famous and sometimes world weary, who were put at ease by George. All the musicians struck up a rapport with the boy from East Belfast, who strummed his first chords in a terrace house, in sight of the world-famous shipyard, where the Titanic was built. Political figures also enjoyed his banter; it's all in this book.

Read and re-live the laughter and wipe away the tears too. It's the inspirational story of a man who understands every aspect of the business we call show. Take a bow, Mr Jones and wait for the standing ovation at the end.

You deserve it.

Liz Kennedy, radio presenter, producer and journalist.

Foreword 2

All of us who have the good fortune to be able to look back on our lives, if we're being honest, will recall both highs and lows, good fortune and tragedy, gains and losses, opportunities taken and missed. In other words, we'll recognise a rich tapestry of experiences, many of which we will celebrate and remember with fondness, others which we'll regret and perhaps dismiss. It takes courage to decide that you've reached a stage in life when you're ready to undertake such an exercise, especially — if like my dear friend George Jones — you're prepared to put the results in autobiographical form and submit them to public scrutiny. However, when George told me that he'd decided to write this book, I wasn't surprised because, having known him both personally and professionally for over thirty years, I was well aware that he had a great story to tell.

Now you may think you already know the George Jones story; after all, he's been one of our best-known entertainers for over half a century … but you would be so wrong. I made the same mistake until in the late 1990s, when I sat down to record an extensive interview with him for a film profile which my production company, Straight Forward Productions, had been commissioned to make for UTV. For the next three hours I was mesmerised as he took me back to his childhood in East Belfast, to his early years as a musician playing for a time in cellar clubs in Germany, to the formation of the legendary Clubsound, to the emergence of his comedy *chops,* to his long and distinguished parallel career as a broadcaster. And all through our conversation what shone through was the strength and inspiration he drew from memories of his parents, his beloved sister Lally, and from his wife Hilary, and their children. The truth is, I realised that I didn't know the half of George's story, and that it's a great story to tell as, dear reader, you will most certainly discover.

Back in the mid-1990s, BBC Radio Ulster management had decided that part of its output should be provided by independent production companies. They asked George, who was already an established presence on the station, if he would agree to his afternoon show moving to the independent sector and, if so, which company would he choose to work with. A few years earlier, John Nicholson and I had both left the BBC to form Straight Forward Productions and it was a great day for us when George walked into our offices and asked us to take on the role of his show's producer. Thus began a ten-year collaboration which has left me with some of the most wonderful memories — how we packed out the Ulster Hall every year for George's Christmas show, how he raised hundreds of thousands of pounds for BBC *Children In Need* through his annual on-air auction, his St. Patrick's Day shows from Sydney and New York, both accompanied by television specials, his interviews with national and international celebrities — Hillary Clinton, Engelbert Humperdinck, Johnny Mathis, Dionne Warwick, all come to mind. But perhaps the most moving memory I have is what happened in the week following the Omagh bomb in August 1998.

The people of Northern Ireland were rightly horrified by the atrocity that killed twenty-nine people and injured over 200. In their despair and anguish many of them turned to BBC Radio Ulster to express their emotion, sympathies and sorrow for and with the people of Omagh. The station's presenters, none more so than George, were inundated with calls from listeners who wanted to go on-air to give vent to their feelings. These calls needed to be treated with considerable care and that is when I began to appreciate a very different side to the George Jones I thought I knew. He instinctively realised that he needed to put aside the happy-go-lucky entertainment presenter's persona and to approach each caller, most of whom were in tears, with compassion and sensitivity. Each show during that tragic week was an emotional rollercoaster which George handled with empathy and humanity. BBC Radio Ulster had become a sort of pressure valve for a shocked and saddened community and George and his fellow presenters certainly rose to the occasion.

Of course, this shouldn't have surprised me because, as I learnt from making that UTV film, George has always had the deepest respect for and commitment to his audiences. He and Clubsound were playing in the Abercorn when that deadly bomb went off in March 1972, and they narrowly escaped with their lives; but it didn't stop them touring all over the province, week in, week out, playing venues on both sides of the political and social divide, bringing laughter and music to people even in the darkest days of the Troubles.

I hope that through the pages of this book you will understand the forces that have driven George at various stages in his life — how he became such a successful musician and composer, a much-loved broadcaster for both the BBC and commercial radio, a very funny comedian and, in recent years, a gifted artist. I can't possibly do justice to the George Jones story in these few short paragraphs ... so may I advise you to turn the page, sit back and enjoy this engrossing account of a life well-lived.

Ian S. Kennedy, past head of programmes BBC N.I. and MD of Straightforward Productions.

Introduction

This morning, I am taken aback by the beauty of the greatest landscaper, as I behold the beauty of the mountains and conclude my book while drinking coffee in Austria, sitting with my wife, Hilary, my long-time love.

I am now the grand old age of seventy-seven; can you believe that? Having first started out in the music industry back in the sixties, which feels only yesterday in my mind, but my aches and pains in the morning tell me otherwise.

I have sung across the world in pubs and clubs on ships and mountain-top bars, performing either in a band or by myself to all diversities of society. The music industry opened the door into the entertainment industry and I have been privileged to broadcast to you on the radio for thirty-plus years. From broadcasting to television presenting, an opportunity arose to host my own documentary series. The world of showbiz has enabled me to travel the globe.

I formed my first band with my school chums, never realising the hits that would be in some of us in the years to come. Time brings change and with each season it brought along a new style, from the good old days of skiffle to rock 'n' roll, and from showband razzle dazzle to cabaret and the hilarity of parody.

Quite a number of you will have heard or even seen Clubsound. I have been performing now with my faithful band Clubsound, for over five decades and have some amazing stories to tell, but I won't spoil them for you now. My long career in broadcasting has given me the opportunity to present shows on Downtown Radio, U105 and BBC Radio Ulster. I have had the privilege of meeting and interviewing a large variety of stars from all walks of life. I have also been blessed to work with some amazing people, many of whom, I am still in contact with today and they have become part of my extended family.

Through it all, I can only say with a tearful eye, I have been blessed through the whole journey to have one woman by my side, Hilary — we've been married for over fifty-three years. Together, we have shared the ups and downs of life; we've always been grateful for life's blessings and not for one second have we taken anything for granted. It is my prayer, that in reading this book you will be inspired to discover your hidden talents and begin to live out your blessings from God.

As you will see, I am just an ordinary guy amazed at the journey of life.

CHAPTER 1

The Early Years

I was born with the name, George Henry Jones in 1945, just after the Second World War. The name Henry, was given to me from my mother's father, Henry McConnell. George was my father's name, George Jones. I have only one sister, who is ten years older than me. She is called Henrietta, but is better known as Lally. Many years ago, Lally carried out research for our family tree. She traced our name all the way back to Cromwell. Two brothers had sailed over in the fifteenth century under Cromwell, in what was known as the Cromwellian War[1]. As part of the Welsh Regiment, if the soldiers did not want to return, then they were offered land to stay. They accepted the offer and settled in the Guildford, Scarva area, in County Down, Northern Ireland. They were known as the Jones' clan and were primarily a farming family, as they lived in the countryside.

At a young age, my father, George and his brother Richie, went to live in Belfast. They both settled in Greenville Street, East Belfast. It was a one-sided street with houses only on that side, while opposite was a huge wall. This backed onto one of the biggest ropeworks in the world, with two back gates leading to the street. Every day at 12 noon, a horn sounded at Belfast Ropeworks as an announcement for the workers to go home for lunch. They were allowed to go through the back gates onto the street. The same horn would also sound at 5 p.m., signalling that it was the end of the working day.

---

1 The Cromellian War (1649–1653) also known as The Cromwellian conquest of Ireland, was the re-conquest of Ireland by the English Parliament, led by Oliver Cromwell.

At every third house, there was a yard with a big gateway. You accessed the yard by going up an entrance between the houses. This opened at the back, behind the houses onto a big yard. My father kept a few lorries in this backyard and there was space to rent out to other people. There was a joiner called George, who believe it or not, had the surname *Joiner,* who rented out the space for a joinery shop. He was famous for building *clinker* rowing boats. He was an amazing craftsman and later on in life, he helped me make my first makeshift guitar which he crafted out of wood. My Uncle Richie lived just three doors down, with a similar set-up; except that he had brought the country with him. It is said that, "You can take the man out of the country, but you can't take the country out of the man." Uncle Richie became content when he brought home a number of pigs. He bred and reared them, and kept them on the street outside his home in the back yard. Uncle Richie paid me pocket money to collect vegetable peelings, potato skins and any other vegetable scraps people had left over, that pigs would love to eat. We would bang on people's back doors, shouting "Yer rufuse! Yer rufuse!" Another way that kids used to make money, was to collect empty glass bottles. People paid a deposit on bottles when they bought drinks such as lemonade. A friend and I collected these bottles from door to door and gave them back to the delivery man in return for a few pennies.

In those days, it was not unusual in Belfast to see cattle walking up and down the street, especially over the Queen's Bridge. There was also evidence of horses frequenting the streets, so it wasn't unusual to keep animals at your house. People kept pigs and goats in their backyards or gardens. Horses were also used for delivering milk from carts, pulling the rag and bone cart, and delivering coal brick. Coal brick was compressed coal dust, for poor people who couldn't afford coal. They were hot-pressed and released steam. Delivery was to streets in poor areas, with twelve bricks being ample for a fire, which was the only form of heating. We didn't have hot water, and at most houses, the toilet was outside. It was a little primitive because there was no kitchen, we had what was called a scullery. In time, we had a *geyser*, a hot-water boiler that was mounted near the sink. We considered ourselves blessed, because we had a yard where we kept the lorries, and we were allowed an extra two rooms. These stretched above the yard in the gateway and adjoined the next house. Therefore, we actually had four bedrooms, whereas most houses only had two. My mother took in a lodger, who I called Uncle Jimmy even l though he wasn't my real uncle. This increased the family income and in the back room, my father had a workshop where he mended things. This was later turned into a music rehearsal room.

From left: Henry McConnell (Grandfather), Dad, Mum, Uncle Harry, Aunt Ella, at my parents'
wedding.

From left: George with David McConnell his cousin.

My father was a general carrier, known today as a haulage contractor. His main area of work was on the docks. In those days, he had two or three different outlets for his contracts. One was serving the biggest ropework in the world — Belfast Ropeworks in Bloomfield Avenue where huge ships came from all over the world to deliver their cargo. Sisal hemp was in demand because it is what is used to make ropes. This was pre-plastic and it came from India. There was the variety of twine, string and rope made there. Everything from fine twine to large ropes for ocean liners was manufactured, and the factory stretched from one street and along another two roads. It was a huge area, with four to five thousand people working there. My father had a contract to deliver large bales of hemp. He loaded the bales with a gigantic hook, which was nearly the same size as him. He went to the docks to get the hemp from the boats. The bales were four and a half feet high by two to three feet square. The hemp was hauled up in big nets and the dockers brought it to his lorry. He manhandled it himself and packed it on to the back of the lorry. I'm a skinny wee fellow compared to him, whereas he was a huge man with big hands; the only thing that I've inherited from him.

He also carried Gallagher's tobacco, which was his main cargo. This raw tobacco came in boxes all the way from Virginia in America and it had this beautiful, sweet smell. It was compressed tobacco, without that horrible smoky smell and he delivered this to warehouses, where it was kept before it went to factories that made cigarettes. He also worked part-time for an Irish bonding company, which supplied the well-known Whitbread's ale. This was delivered from England and he collected crates of ale and took them to a bonding warehouse which they were required to go to because of customs. The company was known as the Ulster Bonding Company. These were his three main contracts.

During the war, when the Blitz was on and bombers targeted the Harland & Wolff shipyard and the Belfast Ropeworks, my father loaded everyone into his lorry and drove into the Castlereagh Hills. Sadly, when the people came back, a number found that their houses had been blitzed.

My father's lorry proved very useful because in his spare time, he helped people move house. Many people couldn't afford to pay for furniture removal companies, so my father offered his flat-bed lorry. Even though it had no sides, we piled people's furniture on to it. Latterly, I went with him, but there were another couple of guys who helped him with what was known in Northern Ireland terms as a *flit* or *flitting*. Consequently, he never stopped, he got up at eight in the morning and worked until six or seven at night. He had two lorries and treated them like babies. He refurbished and repainted them himself; he even refloored them because they were flat-backed.

As a *young snapper*, I travelled with my father on a Saturday morning to collect pigeon hampers. This was for the clubs in East Belfast. They travelled on the train to Cork near the south of Ireland, and were released before they flew back. On our trips in the lorry, we stopped off at the café by the docks. It was known as the ITL — Irish Temperance League. At the age of five or six, I was introduced to my first bacon soda; it was fantastic. In case you don't know, a bacon soda was soda bread made out of flour, buttermilk and a few other ingredients and then a drop of butter combined with couple of prime pieces of bacon. It makes my mouth water thinking about it.

Later on in life, my Dad became a heavy drinker and smoker. Sadly he died from lung cancer at the age of sixty-six. To earn extra money to keep up his habit, he also worked nights as a bookmaker with greyhounds. It was called *Point to Point Races,* which was cross-country racing on a track. He stood holding a board that encouraged people to choose their winner and collect bets from them.

He was a man who did show his feelings, and he expected my mother to care for the children and our home in the small townhouse where we lived in Bloomfield, East Belfast. It was known as Ma Jones' place. He was never really aware of how much money we had, but as a typical East Belfast man, he just wanted food on the table when he came home. My mother was always thrifty with what came into the house and was good at making everything last, whether it was food or clothing. Because there were no such things as fridges or freezers, you had to buy your food daily. There was a fishmonger across the street and I would be sent over to get potted herrings. They were cooked and marinated and then rolled. The bones were taken out, so it was just the fillet with the skin on and it was rolled up. Or, I would be sent to the butcher's to get minced beef or if we had enough money, lamb chops. My father used to love to bring home the vilest things such as pigs' trotters, which revolted me. Another thing he ate was tripe. My mother often sent me to get a pound of tripe and I used to sneak a salt cellar into my pocket and I ate part of the tripe raw on the way home once I had salted it. My friends thought I was nuts, but I loved the taste of this tripe. Yet I wouldn't eat it when it was cooked. This was how life was; you got deliveries often as well as from the breadman, the milkman and, of course, the man selling lemonade bottles among other things. For everything else, you visited your greengrocers and butcher's, daily. Despite our frugal living, we were the only ones in the area fortunate enough to have a phone. You can imagine how popular we were in an emergency. As a working-class family, survival was from hand to mouth.

My Granny Jones died around the time I was born; so I never really knew her. She lived in the Castlereagh Hills and kept cows for a milking business. Near to where she lived, was a place called Orangefield. It was a wooded area with streams and it was our paradise, where, as children, we went to play. It was getting away from an urban area into a rural environment. It was not that far away; we could walk to it in half an hour up Bloomfield Road. It opened out into a large, wooded area, where young kids' fantasies came true. For those moments in our young lives we could be Robin Hood, John Wayne, and play cowboys and Indians or dig trenches and be war heroes. We also used to go fishing and catch small fish which were called smicks or stickleback and we also caught tadpoles. We had this whirl of adventure, and because we were poor, we had to make our own fantasy world. We pretended sticks were guns or used bamboo to make bows and arrows so we could be Red Indians. Do you remember playing these games?

In Winter, because we lived in a very urban environment, we used to throw buckets of water along the street, which froze at night and became our skating rink. My mother used to tear her hair out, not literally, but because we wore out our shoes so quickly skating up and down on the ice. Here she was trying to save money while, so often, we caused her to spend money.

We also played a game at night in the streets called, *thunder and lightning* where we ran up the back alleyways and either kicked the backdoors of houses or knocked on them and then ran away before the people came out. These were the sort of fantasy antics that we created in the environment where we lived. There were no high-powered toys for children born during my generation. Some children had bicycles if their parents could afford them, but our family had to walk to where we wanted to play, so we were grateful for this wooded area that we could reach easily.

My mother came from really good stock. Am I allowed to say that? Anyway, she was a higher level of stock than my father; he was just a country man. My mother's side was called McConnell and, of course, my father's side was Jones.

My maternal grandma was born in Clydebank, West Dunbartonshire, Scotland. Her maiden name was Marian Hoey. She married Henry McConnell, who was in charge of the crane workers of the Belfast Harbour commissioners. My grandfather worked in Canada for General Motors. He and his family lived in Montreal for a very long time.

We have lots of Scottish connections in our family as well as Welsh on the Jones' side. I've got two English Christian names — George Henry, a Welsh surname — Jones, and I was born in Northern Ireland. The Henry came after my mother's father. His son was called Harry, an informal version of Henry, so he was called Henry McConnell as well. My Uncle Harry drove cranes, which loaded coal, and he was head of the crane workers. In those days, the stationary cranes went right along the side of the docks and they loaded everything, primarily coal, which was imported by Kelly's Coal. They were the biggest coal importers and they had their own boats.

Kelly's Coal Yard, Belfast.

My Uncle Harry once saved someone's life. A man threw himself into the sea with the intention of committing suicide. As he was drowning, he started shouting which attracted people's attention. A quick thinker, Harry got into the crane bucket and was lowered down by the crane. He grabbed the man by the shoulders and had to hold onto him when they lifted up the bucket because he was too frightened to get into the bucket. Fortunately, Harry was a weightlifter, so he was a strong man. The story appeared in all the newspapers proclaiming Harry as a hero, which he fervently denied.

A wonderful man, who was kind and generous, though extremely quiet, Uncle Harry married a woman from down country. She lived next to the sea, in a place called Ballywalter. She was called Ella McCracken, and they were devout Christians. My first experience of Christianity came through my Uncle Harry. They had two sons, Jim and David, who were my cousins. I used to play often with my cousin Jim, and when it was his birthday, Uncle Harry was so generous that he not only bought his son a bicycle, but he bought me one too.

Uncle Harry was an introvert, and didn't advertise his faith. Although everyone was aware that he had a faith because it oozed out of him, yet he never enforced his beliefs on anybody. If anyone approached him with a problem or a strong opinion, he would say, "God is the answer." He was a man of few words.

He went to a church on Connsbrook Avenue, which was in desperate need of a church hall, so he built one with his own hands out of wood. Every night when he came home from work, he would work until after dark, building this church hall. There were a few volunteers, but Uncle Harry was the driving force behind the project.

It was Uncle Harry who began instilling Christianity into my sister at an early age. Although, Lally was like me, music first and everything else after. He was recognised from our wider circle as the first one to become a Christian. We all believed in God, and my mother had always encouraged me to believe.

Lally, my warm loving sister was an angel and a second mother to me. My mother died in her arms, my grandmother died in her arms and my uncle practically died in her arms, but he was the last one of the three to go; my grandfather had died earlier on. My sister had lived with my grandmother and my mother, but unfortunately, it came to a point when my mother had to go into a nursing home and that's where she died. As he was dying my uncle grabbed Lally's hand. "What I have, I'm passing onto you," he said. From that moment, Lally became a Christian.

My mother had good breeding, but she married *beneath her*, as was said then. Even though we lived in a working-class family and didn't have much money our main currency was manners. What she instilled in me and my sister, was how to behave and be polite. Little did I know it then, but my mother's teaching laid the foundations for the success of my future career in music and broadcasting. There are three things that my mother taught me to remember in life — never forget where you came from, always remember who you are — and are you ready for it? — hygiene.

We were taught the importance of hygiene. Like many other people at that time, we didn't have a bathroom in our house. Instead, we had a galvanised bath that sat beside the coal fire and mum used to pour in hot water for us to bathe. We were boiled going in and frozen coming out. This would only happen on a Friday and Saturday night. As my sister and I got older, we visited the swimming baths twice a week and had a hot shower at Templemore Avenue in Belfast.

Because she believed in God, my mum encouraged me to go to church. It wasn't long before I joined Cubs and then the Boy Scouts, which led to me attending Sunday School. At ten years old, I joined the Boys' Brigade. I had always wanted to be the drummer in a band, but I was given the bugle. I also hung out with a group of boys who went into the mission halls and Orange halls, to listen to the preacher, listen to the music and sing. We also used to go to local gospel halls and sit in and listen out of curiosity.

Growing up was exciting and Christmas time was no exception. We looked forward to it, but with our family living from hand to mouth, the reality was thrilling yet dreadful. Lally and I grew more and more excited as Christmas Day drew near, wondering what presents we would be given. Then a short while later, we would be deflated because we thought there would be nothing for us on Christmas morning. On Christmas Eve night we heard the bells at St Donard's Church of Ireland ringing across the city. Every year it was the same, we refused to go to bed and stayed up listening to the bells. Outside we heard carol singers walking through the streets singing and chatting with the neighbours. Through the wooden floor boards the Christmas smell rose. Mum cooked a chicken the night before as we couldn't afford a turkey. She let us listen to the carol singers who knocked at the door and then she insisted that we must go to bed, otherwise Santa Claus wouldn't come. Before we went to bed we put out milk and biscuits for Santa and carrots for Rudolph.

Lally and I woke on Christmas morning, each of us debating who should go through the door first to see if Santa had come, and if he had left us something. We opened the door nervously. "You go first," one of us said. "No, you go first," said the other. Disappointment is a terrible thing, especially for children. Slowly but surely, we would look through the ajar door and notice that one of Lally's grey school socks had been attached to the mantelpiece on one side and one of my socks was attached to the other. Carefully, so as not to wake Mum or Dad, we lifted down the socks. There we found an apple, a sixpence and a small bar of chocolate. These were our usual Christmas presents. But some years Dad made us something out of wood; a baby manger or a go-kart.

The home George was raised in

Speaking of carts. I remember my father knew a man called Jim McDowell, who was one of the great Northern Ireland tenors of the time. Jim came to our home often, and each time he called, Lally persuaded me to get up and sing for him, I was only five years old. Lally had been teaching me to sing. She was a wonderful singer, but she never had the tenacity or the confidence to go on stage. She joined the Glee Club, which was a singing group, but she only did it for pleasure. Nevertheless, she would come back all buzzy and sing the songs of the day. Each time Jim visited, he asked me to sing. "What do you want for a present?" he'd then ask me. "A small horse and cart," I replied. But he never remembered to bring one for me.

Impressed by my youthful act, he invited us to his sold-out performance in the Ulster Hall. As we sat there, I felt like a rabbit in the headlights. I was mesmerised by the large hall as I watched people enjoying themselves. With the majesty of the stage and the bright lights, it felt as if I had found home. Unbeknown to me, I did not realise that I was about to be ejected from all my emotional self-appreciation when a voice from the stage cried out.

"There's a young man here tonight who has sung for me many times in his home and I'm going to ask him to come up now and sing."

It was true that it had always been my ambition, even from this young age, to be in a band or start a band, but I did not expect my new-found stage performance to begin like this.

Even though I had heard what Jim had said, it never clicked that he was referring to wee me at nine years old. Even to this day, I'm not sure whether my mum was nudging or thumping me but she was totally mortified. She pushed me out onto the aisle and it became the longest walk of my life. My legs felt numb and weighed a ton as I went up the stairs to the stage. On that stage I performed my *Al Johnson routine,* with my school cap and shorts on.

Once I had finished singing, the crowd clapped. "I'm going to give you something nice for your performance," Jim said. Immediately, I pictured the horse and cart that I had been asking him for. Instead, he gave me a big white piece of paper, which was the old five-pound note. I'm not sure if it was nerves or fear, but I looked at him and instead of saying, thank you, my mouth opened and all I said was, "I don't want that, I want my horse and cart." I screwed up the large five-pound note and threw it at him. The crowd erupted in laughter and I stormed off to my red-faced mum.

It's important to have people around you who believe in your gift, and my sister Lally was surely one of those people. I know you won't likely believe this, but I did lack confidence, and the ability to try new things overwhelmed me.

By the time I was ten, guitars had become very popular on the scene with skiffle music. Everyone wanted a guitar. I had always dreamt of owning one, but my family could not afford one. So, I used some cardboard, cut it into the shape of a guitar and nailed it to a piece of wood. Then, I fixed fuse wire from the cardboard to the end of the wood, and off I went into my own little performance and entertained myself.

As time went by, I became more and more interested in music and it was always drifting into my life, especially through my sister. At this point, she was working as a telephonist at GPO Telephone House in Belfast. There were about fifty or sixty telephone operators, all working in a line. She used to connect all the operators and then she would phone our house. "Go on now, sing a song," she'd say to me. So, at the age of eight or nine I would sing songs to all these operators and I'd crack jokes.

On my eleventh birthday, Lally came round to the house at 9.30 a.m., and there was I still lying in bed, thinking that there was nothing worth getting up for. She stood at the bottom of the stairs and called up to me. "Are you not getting up? It's your birthday." I lay in bed silent. After hearing no reply, she said, "Well, if you don't want your guitar, then that's alright then." My mother said she never saw my feet hit the back stairs of our wee house, I was that excited. I ran down the stairs to go with Lally only to realise that I needed to get dressed.

Lally took me down to the Hollywood Arches, a furniture shop. Because of the guitar boom and the release of colour television, any large store began selling colour TVs and guitars, to make money. With these sales, the shop offered HP (hire purchase),[2] which was a loan instalment plan. Consequently, my first guitar was purchased through HP with my sister's wages. Lally had taken pity on me, when she realised that I needed a real guitar. I left the shop that day walking on water; the box was taller than I was and as heavy as me. That day was the day my fingers touched the string of a guitar and I practised until the blood ran out of my fingers — it was 1955.

Then one day Lally announced that she was going to get married and I was so excited. So, one thing was certain, I for one, would be proud of her on her big day, I could not wait.

As the wedding day came close, Lally asked our Mum when was I

2 It is different from other types of borrowing because you don't own the goods until you have paid in full. Under an HP agreement, you hire the goods and then pay an agreed amount by instalments.

going to be fitted for a suit? At the young age of nine, I didn't think about money. Although my dad wouldn't spend his money on a new suit, he allowed Mum to buy me a second-hand one. Off Mum went to the pawn shop and she picked out a suit for me, and when I tried it on, it looked well on me. I was all smiles — from ear to ear.

The usual warning from any mum came at this stage. "Now you watch that," she said, But, of course, with her running around the house and being busy on the day before, I put my suit on. As I was going through the back door; I had seen a dumper truck and I couldn't resist climbing onto it. Our lodger, my Uncle Jimmy, had a tipping lorry and I slipped between the cab and the actual place that tips up. But hearing my mum shout at me, I slid down the arm of the truck. All I heard was … criiiickk! Mum heard me cry in pain and rushed outside and found me standing there with my ripped trouser leg. My heart sank to the floor as I looked at my trousers and the horror on my Mum's face, I knew there was no chance of me attending the wedding. I couldn't believe it, the very one who had given me so much and sacrificed her time and her money on me; she'd believed in me and I had let her down. It was a sad day as my parents shipped me off to my granny's in Park Avenue and I missed my sister's wedding.

I sat the eleven-plus exam and a technical exam, which allowed me entry to the College of Technology. There I met Roy Kane, who played the drums, Wesley Black, who played rock 'n' roll music on the piano, and Billy McAllen, who played the guitar and became like a brother to me. With Wesley's talent on the piano, we decided that we wanted to form a group, but there was only one problem — we needed to learn how to play the guitar.

A few houses away, I met my friend Billy Dunn, now a pastor, who was also at Elmgrove Primary School. His parents were more well off, so we planned that they could pay for him to have guitar lessons and he would teach us. So, each time he returned from his lessons, he taught us what he had learnt for free. How's that for a deal? Then the next thing, Van Morrison appeared from the adjoining street, and joined in on guitar. That was the beginning of the groups.

School, what can I say? It was not as exciting. Even to this day, I still wonder why a group of lads had to learn about linen looms, weaving, shuttling and spinning. The textile class was the most boring class of all and the teacher matched it. As we said in Northern Ireland, "The dead lice were dropping off him," which means that there was no life left in him; he was ready for death. During the class we used to wait until he fell asleep and then slowly and quietly, we left through the ground floor window and went across the road to the cinema. In those days you could pay to watch a thirty-minute programme. We watched the news and cartoons and then went back, via the window again. Then the bell rang, the teacher woke up and class was over. Our secret, was safe.

Music entered my blood, and what I learnt from Billy and the others, I practised several times over. So much so, my mother often found me in bed sleeping, with my arm over the guitar. And if I didn't fall asleep, I would be practising until four in the morning. My mother would come in and scold me. "You'll wake up your da," she said. Not a great thing to do.

My unpaid manager, my sister, was so impressed when heard us at an event, that she decided to set up another event in Abetta Parade, which was close by. It was an old pigeon hall and the wee pigeon club owned it. Lally, who was a wonderful backing singer, was so enthusiastic when we got our first skiffle group going and we were able to play five or six songs. They were not polished, but we played them and she invited all the neighbours, hoping that they would show up and fill the house; for it would not look good if they did not. She charged everyone thruppence to gain entry and the hall filled up. We played old skiffle songs such as *Bring a Little Water Sylvie* and *It Takes a Worried Man*. However, a few of the neighbours complained. "We'll not be long, my brother's playing," she said to pacify them.

But the biggest surprise that night, was the attendance of my father.

He didn't come wilfully because he did not see music as a manly thing or a way to make money; to him it was not a job. He didn't have a musical note in his head and he didn't know the difference between a fret and a plectrum. However, my mother persuaded him to come and in he came. He sat down near the back, took off his cap and listened. My Mum loved it, she said proudly to people. But like any son, hoping for their father's approval, I could not wait to hear what he thought of the performance. As soon as the show ended, I ran over to him. "Well Dad, what did you think?" I asked him. "It was alright," he replied in his rough voice. "But you'll never get anywhere playing that oul ukulele," he added. As I stood with my only instrument, my guitar not a ukulele, I knew that I would never forget those words. And indeed, I didn't, they have always stayed with me. Yet, as funny as it sounds, it would be as my dad called it, *your ukulele*, that would take me around the world and back, into major concert halls, auditoriums and theatres. That show for my parents and neighbours, was the first professional show that I did.

If Lally hadn't bought me a guitar and if she hadn't known what was in me, I wouldn't have been a musician, because my father would have just had me working and would have said no. But it became my soul, it was in my blood and that was it.

With my school chums around me, we formed our first band called Danie Sands and the Javelins. The band, which consisted of Roy Kane, Billy McAllen, Wesley Black and me, was based around this young girl, Danie Sands, whose real name was Evelyn Butcher. She'd had polio and wore big callipers on her legs to help her walk. She was a beautiful looking girl and had a really amazing voice. We were still at school then, but we managed to secure our first gig at The Strand Cinema, and we performed in what was called a minor's matinée for children, which was on a Saturday. We played during the interval in-between the films. They showed popular films of the day, such as *Flash Gordon*, *Superman* and *The Lone Ranger*. We also entered a competition at the Strand Cinema and played two songs. I sang *Cottonfields* and there were five guitars, a *tea-chest* bass and a washboard. That was what we did in those days and two of the guitar players only knew a few chords, so I'm sure it sounded ridiculous, but I think we thought — this is it. We won ten shillings which would be £50 now. This experience was a strong learning curve, especially as we were still so young in the tooth, as we say in Northern Ireland.

Danie Sands then decided to go her own way as the skiffle style began to disappear because of the increasing popularity of electric guitars. The Shadows were becoming famous, and we decided that we wanted to become more of an instrumental group, so we called ourselves The Thunderbolts.

Van Morrison, an extremely quiet lad whose only desire was to explore music, then to join the band. His father's hobby was to collect records, and Van learnt the music from these. With Van's influence we became a rock 'n' roll band, and played and sang songs made popular by Chuck Berry and Little Richard.

My young teenage years were in the era of black and white television, a long time before Top of the Pops, which started in 1964. I watched Lonnie Donegan MBE, who was born in Scotland and raised in England. For those who aren't familiar with him, he was referred to as the king of skiffle. He was Britain's most successful and influential recording artist before The Beatles. His number one's included, *Cumberland Gap, Gamblin Man, Putting on the Style* and *My Old Man's a Dustman.* But my idol was Buddy Holly; I loved all of his songs. I thought we were alike because we both wore black-framed spectacles.

At the age of fifteen, I left college. Feeling the necessity to contribute to the running of the household and thereby ease my mum's burden, I acquired my first-time position in an office job at a place called Beck and Scott. They were produce brokers. Little did I know that my mum's discipline on manners and cleanliness, qualified and kept me in the job. The boss, happened to be the Lord Lieutenant of Belfast, Colonel Norman Brann OBE ERD. He was the official representative of the queen.

It was there where I learnt that to become the best at something, change must continually take place. My whole etiquette rose to another level in speech, dress, manners and character.

CHAPTER 2

Are You Mad?

It wasn't long before a job became available in the General Post Office, and my sister who was always looking out for her younger brother, arranged an interview for me. It was then that I became a telegram bicycle boy at sixteen years old. Later, I progressed to a motorbike and eventually becoming a postman.

Today, letters and parcels are electronically sorted. But back then, we had to go in early and sort all the letters and parcels by hand. I would fill my bag and get the bus to Old Park Road; my run consisted of twenty streets in that area. Once my bag was empty, I caught the bus and went back to the GPO. After lunch, I sorted and filled my bag again, and jumped back on the bus to complete another run.

Even though we were frustrated at not being able to achieve our goals in music, the good news was that we all had secure jobs. Billy McAllen was working in a builder's yard and our drummer Roy Kane, worked in the shoe department of the Belfast Cooperative Society. This was a huge store with five floors, that everybody called *the Co*. In those days, every household had a *Co book,* which was a form of hire purchase. Parents bought essential items such as school uniforms and shoes, and then paid a little bit off either weekly or monthly. Wesley Black worked in the GPO with me and Van Morrison was a window cleaner during the day.

With The Shadows achieving several number ones, including the famous *Apache* tune, instrumental music was rising through the charts. This caused us to focus not only on our singing but on our playing; we sought to be skilled players. In 1959, I got my first *sunburst* guitar which was a Fender Precision; only three had come into Belfast. Then one night, Van Morrison turned up with his saxophone. Even though at first, he could only play one note, the sound moved us more towards a rock style than a showband style. We were excited, and to make us more professional, we decided to call ourselves The Monarchs. We were now a fully-fledged band and were ready to go.

We had allowed the band to grow to nine members because we wanted to be a showband. Our high-tech rehearsal location was in the back of my father's lorry, in the yard. We played all night into the early hours of the morning, until a neighbour threw something at the lorry or shouted at us. "Hey! I'm trying to sleep."

The Monarchs 1959.

From left: Billy McAllen, George Jones, Roy Kane (drums), Jimmy Law, Van Morrison, Davy Bell, Leslie Holmes and Ronnie Osbourne.

At the weekends, we performed in dance halls and even though we made money, it never crossed our minds how we could build on that to make a decent living. Once we had divided our income between nine members, it didn't seem like a lot. Yes, we were singers and musicians, but at this point, we had no business sense.

At one of our gigs, a bass player from Scotland called Bill Carson listened to our band. He said that he knew an agent called Frank Cunningham who could get us work in Scotland. He advised us to move over there, which is where he claimed, it was *all happening*. He insisted that nothing would happen for us unless we did. Without a second thought, we made the decision to quit our jobs, All except Roy, who decided not to go and continued working in the shoe department of the cooperative. I still remember the night that we were at the gig; I was so excited to go home and tell my mum and dad, unaware of the reaction it would cause.

To my dismay, when I got home and told my parents, my father went berserk. "Leave your job and go to Scotland? Are you mad? You'll be back in a couple of weeks," he shouted. He didn't believe that going professional was a proper job. To leave the security of a steady job and income, made no sense to him. In his mind, what I had decided to do, was complete nonsense. The fact that he didn't appreciate music in his life, made it harder for him to understand. But I was quite adamant that I would be the one to make the final decision. Then a call came from the Scottish agent, to say that we had six weeks of gigs lined up. This was surely our time to go up, up and away.

With our Glasgow boat booked from Belfast to Scotland, it wasn't long before we said our farewells to friends and family in Northern Ireland. When we arrived in Glasgow, we met the manager, Frank, but he didn't have good news. Instead of having six weeks work as he had said, we had two nights work at the weekends. Our excitement dropped to an all-time low.

We ended up living in Frank's house in Glasgow, with him and his wife, his mother and four kids and the six of us. In the summer, I loved it, as we'd play in the garden and the neighbours would come round. We had a lot of fun playing music for them.

After our short stint of gigs, we figured that we'd have to break out on our own. So, we ended up travelling from the north to the south of Scotland, playing wherever we could. When we received any payment, we were faced with the difficult decision of choosing between paying for transport to the next gig or eating food. We chose not to eat; such was our desire for success.

On the way from the Highlands to Aberdeen, we were starving when we saw two Asian girls who were hitchhiking. We decided to pick them up. When they realised that we had no food, the girls asked us to pull over. They jumped out and started to make egg soup with noodles. They cracked some eggs into the noodles, which they had in their bags, and cooked them for us. I never saw a group of men move their spoons so fast; we were literally starving. That night, with satisfied bellies, we had a gig in Aberdeen at the Beach Ballroom.

After touring around Scotland, we were tired and hungry. We thought the only way that we could make ourselves known and become successful, would be to head for the bright lights of London. After all, London was where wannabes were discovered. We naively assumed that we would just bump into people who would promise to make us stars. As we looked at the money we'd received from our gig, we realised that it was now or never. And so, we headed off to London, in search of fame, but for a group of young boys who had never been out of Belfast, the London lights were a whole new world. We pooled our money together for petrol and off we went.

Having no friends or contacts in London, and arriving late on a hot summer's night, we desperately needed to find a place to park up and sleep. We had been driving around for ages, when I said to Harry,

"Just pull in anywhere, pull in here." It was a foggy, smoggy summer's night and as we drove up the road, I spotted a car park sign, so I told Harry to drive to it. It wasn't a hotel, but it would do. He reversed the mini-bus into a car park where we could keep out of sight. We were parked up safely but felt extremely exhausted. In what was becoming normal practice, to keep the smell down inside the mini-bus, we took off our shoes and socks and lined them up along the roof to air them. One guy got some blankets and went to sleep underneath the mini-bus with just his y-fronts on; I dare not tell you who that was. The summer heat made even sleeping outside difficult. As the drummer was six feet four, he'd open the side door and sleep with his feet sticking out while the rest of us were packed inside like sardines and smelt like sardines when we woke.

Early the next morning, we were awakened by a loud, 'Gong! Gong! Gong!' Startled, we jumped up and scrambled over each other. We didn't know what on earth it was. As we clambered out of the mini-bus, we looked at the road above and much to our dismay, there stood a row of very smart-looking gentlemen wearing bowler hats. They were staring at us. We'd parked in the peer's car park at the House of Lords. As there was no security in those days, you could easily park anywhere. "What the hell is that?" one of them said. "Let's get out of here boys," Harry shouted. We grabbed our shoes and socks off the roof and whether we were dressed or not, it was time to get out of there. Harry started the engine and we were off.

As soon as we got our bearings, we drove to the only place we thought we would get noticed — the West End. This was the core of theatres and agencies in London. We thought that if we drove around, someone would discover us. For over a week, we lived in the mini-bus in a car park, starving and with no money. We couldn't get to sleep at night as we were all packed into this mini-bus with all our gear, including our suits. It was unbelievable and the police were always moving us on. To keep ourselves alive, we dipped our fingers into Creamola Foam and for a special treat, drinking chocolate. The caretaker of Leicester Square toilets let us in before it was open to the public, so this gave us a chance to have a wash. Who said show business was easy?

Having been moved on from car park to car park, we were about to give up. "We'd better go home, we're living in a fairy story here," I said. I thought that I would be able to transfer charges to my father's phone as we were the only ones in our street with a phone. I wanted to ring my mum, then she could get my dad to send us some money so we could pay for the boat home. As we were walking around Leicester Square, and I was about to make the call, we bumped into an old friend called Don Charles. We had backed him on a couple of gigs in Scotland. He had a one-hit wonder with *The Hermit of Mystic Mountain*. It crept into the charts and crept out again quite quickly. "What are you guys doing here; are you nuts?" he said in his cockney accent. We told him that we had come to London and we thought that we were going to make it.' He laughed at our expectation that we would get discovered instantly. Then seeing our desperate need to eat, he took us to the Wimpy Bar, which sold fast food such as burgers and chips. There must have been sparks coming out of our knives and forks. "I'm going to help you guys, because you've got a good band," he said. He then phoned his agent and asked if he could do something for us. He arranged an audition and asked if we would put on our suits to allow him to take some publicity shots that he could show around. As instructed, we put on our suits, but as we had been sleeping all squashed together in the mini-bus, our suits had become crumpled. Here was an opportunity to become famous, but we were in a state. He told us to remove the suits immediately, collected them and told us that he would be back in an hour with them dry-cleaned. While he was away, the six of us began to doubt whether he was going to fulfil his word, because at home, dry-cleaning could take up to a week. But as promised, he returned within the hour with our dry-cleaned suits in polythene covers. I was amazed as I'd never seen polythene and the suits looked like new.

After taking us into Hyde Park, he made us hang from trees and took a couple of photographs. He said that he was going to take the pictures and show them to the agency that signed him up. He introduced us to Ruby Bard of Rick Gunnell Agencies. They had signed up a number of big names at the time, including Kenny Ball's jazz band, which was the biggest jazz band at the time, Georgie Fame, who turned out to have many hits, and the Temperance Seven, who were like a roof-top orchestra playing hits of yesteryear. His agent, Ruby, was pleased and loved our band. She gave us an audition and signed us up. Within days, we were booked into American bases in London, because she felt that we were a soul band more than anything. We believed that this was because of Van's influence because he'd taught us these songs out of his father's collection. We were so happy that now we could play music without starving at the same time. Billy, our guitar player, suddenly remembered that he had a cousin in the Woodgreen area in London. Three of us stayed in their house and they arranged another place where the rest of us could stay in a bed & breakfast as lodgers. With accommodation sorted as well, we were really settled.

Within three weeks to a month of us about to go home, we were invited to audition for German club owners, along with ten other bands to perform at nightclubs in Germany. I'd heard of a few of the bands, one had come over to Northern Ireland. To our amazement, we got through with two other bands. We almost couldn't believe it — we were off to the moon.

CHAPTER 3

The Rock 'n' Roll Years

Our old faithful mini-bus would have been able to get us to Dover, but we decided that it was too much to expect it to take us around Germany. After leaving it in Dover, we carried all our gear on to the boat. On the other side, we took the train through France and Belgium into Germany. It never occurred to us that none of us actually spoke or understood a word of German. We arrived in Heidelberg, a fairy-tale town that has a rail tram through the middle of it, a beautiful castle, and the river Neckar curling around it. The next minute, we were sitting at the station in Heidelberg with all our gear not knowing what to do next. Luckily, my mother's teaching had reminded me to have a bit of sense. If I couldn't communicate in German, there was only one thing that I could do. I knew where the gig was meant to be, so I wrote the name of the nightclub, the Odeon Keller on a piece of paper. Keller was the German word for cellar, and it was called the Keller Club because of where it was situated — downstairs. When the next tram came, I jumped on and showed the paper to the driver. When the tram came near to it, he indicated that I should get off and showed me where it was. I knocked on the door. As I was wondering how I was going to communicate, a guy opened the door. As soon as he saw that I was dressed like an Englishman, and greeted him in English, it was okay. I needn't have worried. He went and got the van and I drove straight round to where the rest of the boys were. We collected our gear and went on what we thought was going to be an exciting tour of Germany, singing and playing rock 'n' roll, rhythm and blues, and soul.

Overwhelmed with our sudden workload, we worried about whether we had enough songs. For seven days a week, from eight at night until four in the morning, we played with a break every hour, for ten minutes. We didn't get home until five in the morning and we slept all day until we got up for our next performance the following evening. Whether it was our performance with our Belfast-English accents or the popularity of The Beatles, our band became well known. It got to a point where they asked us to perform a matinée on a Saturday and a Sunday. Therefore, the weekend was the only time that we saw daylight as we had to get up to play the matinées. It was all about the music, there were no drugs. The only drugs that we were given was something to keep us awake. So, by the time we went to bed, we were wide-eyed.

We were staying in a fairly grotty hotel called the Columbia. Each night we walked back to the hotel around 4 a.m., and inevitably someone would forget the keys to get back into the rooms. Because of this, we would regularly be seen scaling the spouting and drainpipes to get into our rooms via the windows; we became experts at climbing walls.

Wes black was the glamour boy of the band and regularly escorted different women home each night. One night he stole a bicycle or in his words — borrowed. It was sitting outside a house on the way home. Apparently he wanted to get back earlier.

He was spotted that morning at 4 a.m. cycling the bicycle up the road and then climbing the drainpipe. The next morning he awoke and behold … the bicycle was gone. It was seen later back outside the house where he stole it from. Now I know what you are thinking, did he or didn't he? The answer, yes, he did. The unbelievable thing is that it went on for a couple of nights, Wes taking the bike and it being returned.

The youth culture in Germany was a contrast to what we were used to back home. When you entered a bar in Belfast, you stayed by yourself or at least with those who came with you; the object was never to mix. Yet, on our first night entering a bar in Germany, our German colleague went in first and started shaking everyone's hand. Naturally, with us following behind, we shook hands with whoever he was shaking hands with. However, as we were sitting drinking, chatting and enjoying ourselves, for maybe our only night off in two weeks, we always ended up being disrupted. There was always someone coming up to us to say *hello* and reaching out their hands to shake ours. We thought it was because of our upcoming popularity, but when we consulted our German friend, this was their custom — to shake the hands of everyone when you entered and left a place.

Wages! What were they? At the end of each week we were handed cash; I don't think anyone of us counted it. The money was spent on food, clothes and drink. We were young and it was all about rock 'n' roll and the girls. Let me tell you a wee secret … frankfurters and chips became the staple diet of the Monarchs.

I enjoyed Germany so much that I started to learn the language over the period of the three months that I was there. Mixing the northern Irish accent with German was an unusual sound. It must have been soft on the ears because girls started to flock to us. As Belfast teenage boys, we felt like pop idols. Most of these bars had American GI's in them, and from midnight onwards, the ladies of the night came into the bars and we saw the young soldiers drifting away with these local German girls. At times when this happened, we would back up against the wall where the speakers were, to protect them, and then the situation would erupt. The local German men did not like their women going off with the American GI's and fights broke out. Glasses and tables were thrown, and sometimes there would even be stabbings.

Unfortunately, our big drummer from Scotland, Larry McQueen, couldn't cope with the drink and started turning up more drunk than sober. I was nominated by the other boys to tell him that he was out of the band. But I couldn't find him to tell him, so I left him a note.

That night at the club where we were performing the door opened. In walked Larry, all six feet six of him. He was facing me and I was a lot smaller. I saw him making straight for me, through the crowd. The rest of the boys also saw him coming, and even though we kept on singing, we wondered how to finish the song quickly. Even though I was on the stage and he was just two feet away from me, my eyes met his. I grabbed hold of the mic stand because there was a chance that I could hit him with it. Suddenly, he stopped. "Am sorry," he said before he turned and walked out of the club. It was then that I realised that whatever tough exterior a man may present to the outside world, it is not a true representation of his character. On the inside, Larry had feelings and though the world saw a hard man, God knew that he was also a repentant man. It would be a while before I realised that God always looks at our heart.

Soon after, I fell in love with a German girl called Ingrid; she was my first love. I only saw her during the day as the GIs were about at night and her father, who was very strict, wouldn't let her out at night. So, I had to settle for just taking Ingrid out for a coffee. When our contract finished in Heidelberg, I had to move to the next location which was Frankfurt. Her parents were very strict and would not allow her to travel. Her father, having been in the Luftwaffe during the war, hated everything English, so I didn't stand a chance.

The Monarchs, Ariola Studios, Cologne, Germany.

Upon our arrival in Frankfurt, we got ready to play our next gig at the Storyville Jazz Club, only to find out that our audience had changed. They were from a different era in age and music tastes. Our repertoire had begun to widen because of the American GI's, who enjoyed blues and soul. We had moved from Heidelberg which was the American sector and this was in West Germany, which was divided between the Americans and the British as it wasn't that long after the war. When we were playing in Heidelberg, it was nearly all American music, which was rock 'n' roll. We were now coming into the British sector and they wanted up-to-date Merseybeat groups, including The Beatles who were in the charts. We were playing what we termed was the rock 'n' roll that we knew, but this was now the British sector and they wanted songs from the British hit parade. Because we had been working around the clock and sleeping through the day, we were just focusing on our own songs and hadn't really noticed the change of music style that was happening around us with The Beatles' songs. We had heard of them, but we didn't take heed of them. When the club began to request songs from the United Kingdom, we knew that we had to change and change quickly or risk losing the crowd.

With the departure of our Scottish drummer Larry, we decided to bring over another drummer, called Oliver Trimble, his nickname was King Oliver. We also asked Roy Kane, who had stayed in Belfast, to come back and be our lead singer, because he had sung a lot of the vocals. Having stayed in Northern Ireland, they had become *au fait* with all The Beatles' songs and the British hit parade in Northern Ireland. We needed to change our repertoire to suit the clientele who were asking for more British hits. Within days, we had learnt all the tracks and were ready to go.

Once we mastered the UK chart singles, the Frankfurt performances became a success. The next stop on our tour was Cologne. When we arrived, we were in awe of the sight of the huge cathedral. We decided to visit it and I remember thinking that it was the finest building I'd seen with its amazing architecture and skilled carpentry. What struck me most was that the people had built such a large and wonderful place for God. Now, I wasn't a God-fearing person or a Christian, but the thought of people devoting themselves to building such a fabulous place, did cause me to think about God.

One night in Cologne as we were performing in a dark room filled with smoke and only a little light, I saw the figure of a man standing at the back, who I could only describe as Dracula. This dark-haired man had on a cloak, the collar of which stood up. This not only reminded me of Dracula but also of Transylvania, where Dracula is said to have originated from, and which is not far from Germany.

With every song that I sang, I scanned the room and kept a watchful eye on *Count Dracula*. We came to our break and I went and sat down at the table to have a beer. "He's really weird looking," one of the guys said. And then the next minute he looked at me and nodded, as if someone was behind me. "Cover your neck," said another guy. I was about to escape to the bar, when this hand landed on my shoulder. I'm not sure if I swallowed a mouthful of drink or spat it across the table. Then I heard him speak. "Can I have a word with you?" As I turned around slowly, I realised that I didn't have an option when a six-foot German Dracula was accosting me. All I could say was, "Okay." I got up to go with him and I heard the boys whispering. "Take garlic with you," one of them said.

He introduced himself as Roland Kovacs and said that he was a jazz piano player, second in command, next to the owner of CBS in Germany. "I could make you a star here," he said. But all I could think was that I'd heard all that before. "I want you to make a record for me," he said and went on to say that he'd written two songs and that he wanted me to be the one to record them. "What do you mean?" I asked. "I want you to sing them by yourself," he replied. I explained that if the band was not included, then I wouldn't do it.

So, the next day he arrived with the two songs and asked if the band would perform them for a recording. They were not great songs, so we put in an arrangement with our own style and produced an A side and a B side of our first single. We recorded them at the Ariola studios with Van playing saxophone, Wesley Black playing piano, Keen Oliver on drums, Billy McAllen on guitar, me on bass and lead vocals and Roy Kane on backing vocals and tambourine. We completed the recording of the two tracks in one day.

The Monarchs, 1963 record release.

From left: George Jones, Billy McAllen, Harry Mac, Wes Black, Lawrie McQueen

Front from left: Van Morrison and George Hetherington.

The next day, Roland called me and invited me to lunch. He turned up in a fancy Porsche. During the meal, he looked at me and said, "I think you've got great potential. Come and stay with me in Germany, drive my Porsche; I will look after you and make you a big star." Suddenly, alarm bells started going off in my mind that this guy was getting too close and there was something not right. Oh, if ever the ground could open, I prayed it would be now. I was stammering, as I ended that conversation and reverted back to the music. I thought here I am, a young lad, just a teenager, and I could hear my mother's voice in my head saying, "No, you're coming home." "Look Roland, I've decided to go home. Just pay me what you've paid the guys in the band," I replied. He reached into his pocket and handed me fifty pounds for each member, which was a lot of money back then. I never heard from him again while we were there. Our German tour had come to an end and it was time to return to Belfast.

After the incredible experience that we'd had touring Germany, it was with mixed feelings that we began our journey home as we wondered what lay ahead of us. We travelled back the way we had come and were relieved to see that our old mini-bus, which had taken us around Scotland and down to London, was waiting for us at Dover. After piling into the bus, we drove across England to the next port, where we sailed back to Northern Ireland.

My father was waiting in his flat-bed lorry when we came off the boat at Larne. All nine of us climbed onto the back of the lorry, including our American friend, Jim Storey. He had decided to come home and see Ireland, as he had sung some songs with us when we were in Heidelberg. There weren't any seats or seat-belts, we just huddled up together with all our gear. Health and safety had not yet been introduced, otherwise we wouldn't have got away with it. We drove through Belfast, navigated around cattle, and crossed the Queen's Bridge to those bumpy cobbled streets as we held on to our gear with all of our might. It was a bit of a hairy ride, but those were the days. The American had never seen such professionalism. It was so surreal for him. He must have been saying to himself, what have I got myself into?

When we finally arrived home, my mum was pleased to see me safe and well. After a few days of settling in, she decided that it was time to sit me down and counsel me. She explained that if I was going to have a career in music, then I needed to earn some money and contribute to the running of the home. My dad was not so subtle. "If you're staying in music, you've got to make your music pay. And if not, get yourself a real job," he said.

It wasn't long after when a parcel arrived with a German stamp on it. After opening it to see what it was, I found twelve singles with covers, with my photo on them. *Georgie and the Monarchs* was written on the covers. "Congratulations, your record has been released," said the letter inside. A few weeks later, I received a telegram. "Your record is doing very well," it said. Shortly after that, another telegram arrived with the news that the record was now in the German top ten. Our single, *Boohzoo Hullygully*, reached number five in the German charts, in 1963. The hullygully was a dance like the twist that came from America. We had a B side as well and that was called, *Oh Twingy Baby*. This guy really did want to make me a big star.

When I look back, the whole London and Germany adventure was a time of change in my life. If we hadn't had met Don Charles, out of the blue in Leicester Square, the band would have gone home and dispersed into other bands and not stayed as The Monarchs. If we had not gone to Germany and been attracted to the blues' scene, I don't think that any of us could have afforded to go back to London again. I can honestly say that this was a really pivotal part in my life. I really believe that meeting Don in among thousands of people in London was a God-inspired moment. Just when we had given up all hope and decided to go home, God had his hand on our lives and inspired that meeting with this one guy.

CHAPTER 4

The Showband Years

Van Morrison and Billy McAllen decided to go back to London but I stayed at home. Music was in my blood now, but I was conscious that I needed to earn money from it. It was then that the showbands came on to the scene. It was an unforgettable time with nearly eight hundred showbands throughout Ireland, ploughing their way into every dance hall. Because of the experience I had gained in Germany, I was asked to join the Stan Lynn Showband, which gave me a steady income. The brass section took on a whole new meaning when I played Ray Charles and similar genres in Germany. The band became very popular and certain bands were creating particular styles, for example — Indians, cowboys and cadets. Because there were so many bands, each one was trying to be different and looking for a gimmick. Very soon, Billy and Van decided to return home. Billy was totally dissatisfied with the way the music was changing, from The Beatles to the long hair of the Rolling Stones and The Who. Billy joined our band, but Van found another band that would travel with him. It was called Them. Van had always been into the blues' scene and was still very much influenced by the blues and what he had heard in London. He didn't express a wish to join a showband and alternatively became a pioneer of promoting the blues' scene in his hometown. He was one of the instigators of setting up a club called the Maritime Blues Club. It was an ex-sailors' club, which catered for all the blues' bands and beat groups that didn't want to be showbands. The rest they say is history with Van, who was making an extremely successful career out of his talent and songwriting.

To help increase the momentum, we looked for that gimmick in the Stan Lynn band; we thought that it was time to change our image. We decided to call ourselves The Silhouettes and amusingly, we dressed all in black with knee-length black boots and a black mask similar to a balaclava, only more decorative. I think that Darth Vader got his idea from us, and this was before the Troubles.

Bands had press kits and naturally, our photos were on posters and bills. On the images, we were each given a number printed on our masks above our heads and no one could distinguish between us except by our numbers. We ended up looking like numbered batmen dressed in black.

Travelling throughout the island of Ireland was very similar to working all the hours we had in Germany. We left very early in the morning to arrive at the dancehall. After setting up our equipment, we'd have food, although if it wasn't provided, then we'd go without. We would then get changed before the arrival of the dancers. I remember playing in the Abbey Ballroom in Drogheda, a town in the Republic of Ireland. We proceeded to do the usual routine of getting ready before the dancers came and when they arrived and we came on to the stage, the crowd had never seen anything like it. I don't think that they could quite believe their eyes. Seven so-called batmen were trying to engage the crowd with a normal performance. But would anyone dance? No, not one.

The hall began to fill with smoke, people were having more to drink and then one by one they started to move towards the stage. They were not joining in to dance, they wanted to know who these masked singers were. As a matter of fact, I think that they were having a competition with each other because they had our photograph cards in their hands. They were obviously trying to distinguish who was who, but I couldn't help thinking that they thought it was an April Fool. Fascinated, they gathered around us, looked us up and down, yet in our wee minds, we did not detect the issue. By the end of the night, the crowd had grown in number, and they were all standing tightly packed in front of the stage. We did not realise that they were so eager to see who was behind the masks, until in the end, they pounced on us. We had to run for our lives and escape to the dressing rooms before they ripped off our masks and exposed our identities. I'm unsure whether it qualified as mass hysteria such as the Beatles endured, but we barely got out alive.

After my stint in the Silhouettes I went to Germany a second time for a short period. At that time, Irish bands toured regularly, and Billy and I had both been in The Silhouettes and so had Roy. We were given a month's contract in Germany, in Keil, north of Cologne. It was in a club called The Star Pallast. We played there and wore jackboots and they thought it was amazing. They had never seen brass in a band. It was then that I contacted Ingrid, my first love. But her father wouldn't let her go to the club where the Americans were, because he had a thing about English-speaking people.

At the time, there was one stage in Belfast and thirteen ballrooms. We became the resident band in one of these ballrooms, and it was called Romanos. Of course, that was after we abandoned the Batman suits and dressed just like an ordinary-style band. We had great experiences as the resident band because a lot of the big sixties' groups used to visit and we had an opportunity to see a lot of these top groups such as The Kinks, Dave Dee, Dozy, Beaky, Mick and Tich and The Searchers.

In 1965, I received an opportunity to join another band. The band was fronted by a guy who had been an actor on the Crossroads programme on television called Benny. He was the original Benny, who played guitar on the television series. He was a good-looking guy with blond hair and became an instant television idol on the programme. He had decided to come to Northern Ireland to do an initial tour because he could sing as well as play the guitar. So, three or four of us got together and formed a backing band for him. He proved to be a big hit, which prompted him to stay and form a proper showband, called The Tara.

Soon after, an opportunity arose when the original drummer, Desi McCarthy, who we had in the Stan Lynn Showband, left and joined the famous Dave Glover showband. Their bass player Jackie Flavelle, decided to leave and join Chris Barber's jazz band, and created a bass vacancy, so Desi said to Dave Glover that I should be the one to play bass. In 1966, I left the Tara showband and accepted the offer of playing in one of the top showbands in Ireland, The Dave Glover showband. I played for six nights a week for the next three years. During that time, I felt that I was with one of the best bands in the north. He always managed a good band, and we were in the premier division.

Dave Glover who formed the showband, was a very tall man, and because he knew what he was looking for in an act, he was a hard taskmaster.

So, there I was, trekking the roads throughout Ireland nearly every night, but we were not earning much money. For four nights we were paid forty pounds and for every extra night that we played, we would earn just ten pounds. Therefore, we couldn't afford to book into a hotel or a guesthouse. Wherever we played in Ireland, we had to travel home in the early hours of the morning. Or if we played in Portrush on a Friday night, we would travel over three hundred miles to be in Cork the next day to play.

On most mornings, I was dropped off at my parents' house and as I came through the door, my dad would be going out to work. Yet, my body would come alive as the smell of an Ulster fry[3] hit my nose. My mother always cooked that for me, knowing that we often didn't eat while on tour. After eating the Ulster fry, I headed to bed, before being picked up later in the day in the band wagon ready to perform all over again.

In the days of the showbands, one thing that never came up on the journeys was the question of whether you were a Catholic or a Protestant. Musicians seemed to live in a very pleasant neutral world in that respect. Regardless of where the event was held, in Portrush or

---

3 The Ulster Fry is considered to be the ultimate breakfast food and is Northern Ireland's favourite dish. Consisting of fried sausages, bacon, eggs and tomatoes, with the addition of griddle-baked soda farls (quarters) and potato bread, fried until golden crispy on the exterior, and tenderly fluffy on the interior with beans. Now, fried mushrooms, white pudding, black pudding can be added but hardcore traditionalists might reject these.

Dublin, if there was one thousand in attendance or three thousand, religion never played a part. Musical entertainment, from the public's perspective, was an escape from the religious issues that dominated the daily lives of people in Ireland.

I remember one night playing in the Arcadia Ballroom in Cork. We very rarely went on stage before eleven at night, therefore a relief band would always play at the start; they were called the warm-up band. Desi McCarthy and I decided that we wouldn't stay to see the warm-up band and went out to grab something to eat. After we'd eaten, we decided to head back to the ballroom, and on our way back, I heard this wonderful guitar playing coming from the ballroom. "Gosh, I've got to go and hear that," I said. So, we went in and walked up to the balcony. There were about three thousand people in the ballroom and three people on the stage, one of which, was an amazing guitar player, playing blues and rock. Of course, I immediately thought back to my time in Germany, when I was loved that music. I was awe-inspired as I looked at him. All the while they were playing though, the crowd were shouting, "We want Dave Glover! We want Dave Glover!" which was the name of our band. After all, they had come to see a showband. I was totally bemused by the whole thing and made my way to the stage and grabbed the young lad. "I have never heard guitar playing like that, it was wonderful. Do you live here?" I asked him. "Yes, I live in Cork," he replied. "Well, you're wasting your time here, you'd be better going to London where there's a big blues' scene or maybe go up and meet a guy who I know well, called Van Morrison, who started up a blues' club, the Maritime Blues Club in Belfast." Lo and behold, this guy did go to the blues' club. And little did I know that this guy would go on to become one of the most renowned guitarists and blues' singers. He, of course, was Rory Gallagher, who is one of the world's greatest guitarists.

Speaking of the world's great guitarists, when I came back from Germany with The Monarchs, I was asked to go and help the grandson of my father's business partner. He wanted to learn how to play the guitar.

Quite willingly, I agreed and went up to a little seaside bungalow in Millisle village, a few miles from Belfast and found this young lad, about ten or eleven years old. I tried to teach him what I knew about playing the guitar. I went two or three times, but he always complained about his fingers hurting. I tried to tell him that if he wanted to be a good guitarist, then he would have to work through it. After a few visits, I spoke to my father, who asked me how he was getting on, and I made one of the world's greatest understatements of all time. "That kid will never be a guitar player," I said. But astonishingly, he turned out to be one of the world's greatest — Gary Moore. So, it turns out that I taught Gary Moore his first four or five chords on the guitar. However, I don't claim, of course, to have discovered him, but I was responsible for instigating the very beginning of his guitar playing.

One issue that did affect the audience, was how we dressed. Showbands were frowned upon as they wore smart suits and ties. I had come a long way from dressing all in black. This didn't please the blues and beat groups because they wore leather jackets and T-shirts, and they didn't like us dressing smartly. One of the reasons we dressed in suits was that a lot of our crowds were urban or from *down country* and they loved their waltz and quickstep as they believed that they were dancing to a *proper* dance band.

Dave Glover Showband – George on right

In 1967, when I was in the Dave Glover showband, we played quite regularly in a place called Capronis. This family had a name for making a famous ice-cream. Mr Caproni had a beautiful ballroom in Bangor. We played there once a month; it was really popular and always packed. There was this girl who I took a fancy to, but she was always with her boyfriend. The guys in bands were always trying to catch the eyes of the girls dancing, but I could never catch her eye. At that time, I was going with a girl who I met up with occasionally, but it was not serious. I suspect you might be wondering, what was I thinking?! Going with a girl but looking at another. But I was young and foolish, like many other lads at that time. However, inside my heart, I knew that I wanted this girl to be mine. I knew that she was the one; she just didn't know it yet.

My desire to play in Bangor grew and grew more each week. It was not just the music now that was whetting my appetite, I longed for this girl to be with me. Each time we played there, I would look out for her until I saw the boyfriend following her and then my heart would become deflated. Until one night, she arrived with two girlfriends and no boyfriend. Ever the lad at heart, I thought this was my opportunity and best chance.

When the evening of music ended, the majority of the people would still hang around, chatting and getting to know each other. For weeks I had been practising what to say if the opportunity ever arose, and here I was standing just two feet from her. I sidled up to her and said the corniest thing. "Would you do me a big favour and tell me your name?" It wasn't very romantic. "Hilary," she replied. I asked for her phone number and she seemed happy enough to give it to me. We started chatting and laughing and it turned out that she'd split up with her boyfriend. "Would you mind going to the pictures?" I said. "Alright," she said after thinking about it. We'd planned it for a Wednesday night, but being a typical man, I couldn't wait and I decided to contact her on the following day, which was Sunday. I was earning good money at the time in the showbands, so I could afford a car. I drove up to her parent's house where she lived, but I hadn't enough courage to actually pull up at the front door. So, I stopped at a phone box close to her home to make the call. There were no mobile phones in those days. "Would you like to go out for a meal to an Italian restaurant on the High Street in Belfast?" I said when she answered. "Well, I've just washed my hair, it's in curlers and my friend's here," she replied. "Well, I was just driving round in Belfast and I was thinking that I'd love a meal and there's a place that's just opened called The Steak House," I replied. It was one of the first places that cooked spaghetti bolognese. "How long will it take for you to get here?" she asked. "Well, I'm actually parked outside your front door," I stammered. When she got into the car, she said that she had just had dinner but offered to go with me to the restaurant. This wasn't quite what I imagined, but here I was eating a full dinner in a restaurant with Hilary sipping coffee as slowly as she could to allow me to eat my dinner. Romantic or what?!

When I brought her back home, she told me about her parents Bill and Dolly Roy, who lived in a beautiful apartment on the Ormeau Road. Her mother was an international champion bowler and her father was a top Belfast accountant. He was a very astute, quietly spoken man who smoked a pipe. Whether it was his training or his nature, he looked at everything carefully before he made decisions — as I was to find out later on.

Our second date didn't go to plan, because I had been seeing this other girl on and off. I invited Hilary to come and hear me play at the Floral Hall Ballroom. Lo and behold, to my horror I didn't realise this other girl had spotted Hilary and me coming in, and she started jostling and harassing Hilary on the dancefloor, out of jealousy. I had just met Hilary, but I hadn't told her that I was going out with this girl, and to my detriment, Hilary found out the hard way. But luckily there was another guy in our band who had his girlfriend with him. She was a bit of a toughie and she came to Hilary's aid. She protected Hilary and told this girl to clear off. But at the end of the night, Hilary said to me, "What are you doing bringing me here?" I thought, oh no this is the end, but we smoothed it over and then everything settled down and we continued going out together.

We had been going out for a year when, Hilary's sister Janice, announced that she was getting married. The news prompted me to consider marriage as well. I asked Hilary if we should get married? Her response was that I would need to ask her father. Therefore, I knew I had to plan this carefully.

It's not as common now, but in those days the father of the bride paid for the wedding. With a wedding already planned in that household with Janice, I knew our chances were slim. I was a long-haired, skinny guy with few job prospects and I was about to ask Hilary's father who was always smartly presented and dressed in a suit, for the hand of his daughter.

I approached her father. "I was wondering would you give me the honour of taking Hilary's hand in marriage? And would you please give us your blessing?" I said.

I hadn't thought it through too much, for when I asked him, he was taking a puff of his pipe and I think the smoke got caught in some of his chambers as he coughed and spluttered and tried to pull himself together. "I think you need to wait for a wee while, until we get Janice's wedding over," he replied. And that was it, we had to wait for a whole year. Then I asked him again. "I'll agree to the wedding, but you need to get a *proper* job," he replied. My father's sentiments all over again

We got married in August, 1969. The wedding was in St Jude's Parish Church of Ireland, because Hilary's family were in the Church of Ireland, Ormeau Road. We had a reception in Knocknagoney House Hotel, which is actually a police headquarters now. We had a wonderful day with all the family, but strangely, there was no music because it wasn't planned. We didn't have time for music and entertainment, whereas nowadays, music and entertainment go on into the night. After the meal, everyone sat chatting and there were the usual speeches. But we had to leave straight after and drive to Dublin to catch a flight.

George and Hilary on their wedding day.

The timing of the wedding was maybe not the best as the Troubles broke out during the same period that we were on our honeymoon. As Hilary and I travelled in a taxi to Dublin airport, we cut through Cromac Square, in Belfast, and you'll never guess what was happening ... there was a gun battle going on and suddenly we were driving through it. I pulled Hilary on to the floor of the taxi as the bullets flew. Great start to a honeymoon, eh? From Dublin, we travelled to Majorca for a two-week honeymoon. In those days, Majorca was not a very established place, and there were only two hotels in the area. We stayed in a place called El Arenal, and the hotel was called Aya. Would you believe that the holiday, including the flights, only cost us ninety pounds for two weeks?

That was the start of what would turn out to be our travels around the world. Since then, our lives have been a series of ups and downs like a rollercoaster; sometimes good, sometimes bad. We've been down and out a couple of times in my musical career, but together we came through. Yet I wouldn't have met my wife if I hadn't been in the band. All through my career, Hilary has been there, sometimes reluctantly, other times selflessly and occasionally without saying a word. But through it all, I have to say, that there is no one like her. Going back to the night in Capronis, to this day, I knew that she was my girl and now she knows it.

Our first house together was in Pottinger Street, in East Belfast, next door to my sister. Admittedly, it was my sister who got us the house, as she persistently asked the rent man if any houses were coming up on the street, and he told her when they were, as they were quite hard to acquire in those days. We moved into a huge, three-storey Georgian house, that cost only one pound per week. It was a beautiful house and it had an annexe built onto it. There we were, and it was just over two years since we'd met. We had our own house and had begun our married lives together.

To honour my promise to Hilary's father, when we the returned from our honeymoon, I applied for a rep's job, a travelling salesman with Campari. Yes, the same name as the drinks company. This was a company that produced all types of clothing, including industrial wear, such as coats, jackets, boots and leisurewear. They even sold camping equipment and inflatable boats. I had to go to London for my interview, but it was worth it as I got the job. They were a Jewish company, and my immediate boss was called Benjamin Benjamin — double name. He was also the main overseer of Belfast. In Belfast, I was given a small van packed with all the various products that they sold, and I was ready to begin selling. They started me off with five contacts and in my first year, I built it up to almost a hundred trading accounts.

From that point on, my job just kept getting better and better. New accounts were opened and the demand became greater. Then one day we had a new arrival; it was what was known as the parka. These were khaki-coloured coats which had hoods and some had fur trim. One of the larger accounts was a shop called McAnultys in Smithfield and every time I went back, he placed massive orders for these parkas. "Why are you selling so many parkas?" I asked the owner one day. He just winked at me. "Think about where I live out here George, *the boys* need them," he replied. It was then that I realised that both sides of the paramilitaries, the UDA, UVF and the IRA were purchasing these parkas as their set uniforms with masks and balaclavas. It was quite surreal as I was buying them from a Jewish company in London and selling them to a Catholic shop in Smithfield markets. We were selling them in their hundreds. The Jewish people couldn't understand why they were selling so fast. "Don't ask, just send them over," I said. Our phone was constantly ringing as more and more orders were being placed by shops. Everyone was trying to make money out of these parkas. So much so, I decided to order a container load of them, without really thinking where it was going to go. It took many trips up and down the ladder to fill the attic in our large house. When that was full, we built a storeroom onto the back of the house. But it wasn't long before all the parkas had sold out again. Please don't blame me for those uniforms.

I stayed in that job for two years, but I was yearning so much to get back to music and be in a band.

Belfast shops sold out of Parkas.[4]

---

4 Sunday News, June 11, 1972.

It was a couple of years earlier in 1969, that the music scene had taken a quick change and gone from ballrooms to cabaret clubs. I think people had got tired of dancing. It was either that or they were afraid to go out in large numbers to the ballrooms because of the Troubles. Music had become popular again and I was offered a job in one of the main cabaret clubs in Belfast called the Abercorn; the resident band had asked me to join them. By then I had one hundred and twenty-five contacts for Campari in Northern Ireland, so I asked if they could give me another man, meaning that I would be the overseer and then we would split the areas. Unfortunately, they wouldn't agree as they said I was doing a great job, but it was hard work to cover the whole of Northern Ireland. Reluctantly, I explained that I had made the decision to leave the company, as I wished to return to being a musician, full-time, and that my wife, Hilary, was in agreement. I knew I was earning just as much money at night as I was during the day. So, I also spoke to Hilary's father, for his blessing, that I was going to leave Campari and he accepted it.

CHAPTER 5

The Beginning of Clubsound

When I left the sales job, the band that I joined in the Abercorn, was a split from The Dave Glover Showband, called The Professionals. It had become a cabaret band, and that's when the style changed. Cabaret had really begun to take off and I became not just a musician, but a compere as well. I brought some of my comedic style to the show by telling a few jokes I had in my repertoire from my boyhood and Lally's training.

The band was full of great guys; Tony Morellis, Gerry Rice, Tommy Smith and George Bradley who were all great musicians.

That lasted for a couple of years then The Professionals split up and Dermot O'Donnell, the owner of the Abercorn, approached me and asked if I would form a new band. The idea was to continue entertaining the public when we could, as a source of comfort and escape from the horrors of the Troubles, that had become commonplace. I formed a band and we began rehearsing. We practised and rehearsed for six nights a week, until the night of our first performance, when we suddenly realised that we had overlooked an important matter. We had forgotten to think of a name for the band, until Dermot brought it up. "What's the name of the band?" he asked. "We don't have a name. Do you have any suggestions?" I replied. "Well, you're playing in the Abercorn Club and you make a sound, call it Clubsound," Dermot replied and it was as flippant as that. Little did we know that we would become a legendary band. That name has lasted for fifty-three years and it has turned out to be one of Northern Ireland's biggest bands.

By then the Troubles were touching everyone's lives in strange ways all over Northern Ireland. My friend, Wesley Black, from The Monarchs, had become a devout Christian, following in the footsteps of his mother and father who were also devout Christians. Unfortunately, his marriage to Karen broke up and his daughter went to live with her mum. On one occasion, after he collected his daughter from her school because she was missing her dad, they went for a walk and chatted about her life. When he dropped her off at home, he said an unusual thing to Karen. "Is everything alright with you in life?" Karen thought it was very strange, and he duly said his goodbyes. He headed down the road and called into the local chippy. While he was walking along the road, eating his fish and chips, and minding his own business, he bumped into two gunmen who were trying to escape over the wall. When they knocked Wesley's fish supper out of his hands he grabbed hold of one of them. "What are you doing?" he asked. Without warning, they shot him and ran off. They had murdered him in cold blood.

Onlookers gathered around Wesley as he lay on his stomach, bleeding profusely. A plain-clothed soldier pushed through the crowd to help. He turned Wesley over, but in doing so, caused the blood to gush even more. He was pronounced dead before the ambulance arrived.

As the Troubles increased, travel around the country was coming to an end, especially at night; it was just too dangerous. Belfast centre was being destroyed, and in turn, this was forcing the people out to stay within their own small communities. Clubs were a target because that's where people congregated for entertainment. Sadly, they were gradually being closed down, either because of bombs or threats. However, Abercorn's owner Dermot, was determined to stay open, and on a Saturday, they had a matinée that attracted up to two hundred and fifty people. Posters were displayed to advertise the different acts including Clubsound, who had become really successful as the resident band in the Abercorn.

Even so, security measures increased and bags were searched at the door. Whether you looked suspicious or not, and regardless of whether you were a man or a woman, you were searched without question. With bomb scares becoming more frequent, we needed to come up with a way that our band and the staff could communicate with each other without causing panic. For example, if there was a bomb alert, we needed to know how to end the show quietly and get everyone out of the premises without causing alarm.

A member of the Fire Service came up with the idea that whenever a bomb was in the area or in the building, the resident band in each club, would have what they called a *fire tune,* but at that point we didn't know about this at the Abercorn.

On most Sunday afternoons, we rehearsed with the star act for the following week. These were legends such as Frank Carson, Roy Walker and Jimmy Cricket, who would perform every night the following week. During one of our rehearsals, the door opened and two firemen entered carrying a clipboard. We explained that we were in the middle of our rehearsals and politely asked if we could be of any help. "We need to know what your fire tune is?" one of them said. Completely ignorant of this new requirement and under a time constraint to prepare the show, Eddie McRudden spoke up quickly. "Look, we're very busy. Just put down that our fire tune will be *Three Blind Mice.*"

So that was it, the fire tune for the Abercorn, was established as *Three Blind Mice.* When the alert was given, instead of alarm bells going off, we immediately began to play the familiar nursery rhyme. Only the staff in the building knew what this tune meant, but they always stopped stop what they were doing immediately and took up positions at the doorways, hallways, and nearest exits.

Years later: Trevor Kelly, Dermot O'Donnell and George Jones.

Dermot was the owner of Abercorn and the person who named Clubsound.

I had been trying for years to bring my friend, Max G Beesley, a brilliant drummer and a great impressionist, from Manchester to the Abercorn to perform. His son was the well-known actor, Maxton Beesley. Like many names, he was terrified of coming to Northern Ireland for fear that he would be shot or bombed, and that kept him away. Nevertheless, he eventually decided to come and stayed with us in our home when he used to keep me up until three or four in the morning. He stayed up with me and practised the Belfast accent because he was an impressionist and he wanted to get it right. He played at the Abercorn all week and the audience loved him. By the time Saturday came, he had really begun to enjoy himself. "Well, it's alright here," he said. It was the matinée show and he was ten minutes into his act, doing an impression of Ken Goodwin. He had a line where he said, 'I'm getting tired now so I'm going to go." And on this particular occasion, when he got to that line, "BANG!" a bomb went off. It was a large explosion, but it all happened in slow motion. The entire front of the building was blown out. The bomb had apparently been placed in the Abercorn restaurant below the club. It was the first incident with major fatalities and terrible injuries in Belfast City Centre, during the Troubles. The building upstairs, was full of smoke, fire was breaking out, there was shattered glass and everyone was in a panic. Max, well he just went to pieces and collapsed. What we thought was smoke, was actually dust filling the air. It was pouring out of the carpet that had been impregnated by years of Guinness being spilt on it. Little did we know it was the carpet that saved two hundred and fifty lives because the army bomb squad told us that it weighed only two and a half pounds. If it had been a couple of pounds more, then the floor wouldn't have held, because it was the carpet that held the floor together and it was what took the impact. If the floor had fallen through, then it would have been an absolute tragedy as over two hundred people would have died. Sadly, some people did lose their lives, others lost limbs and many were badly injured in the restaurant below. Pandemonium ensued as people ran around, a number were drunk. I grabbed the microphone, which was thankfully still working through the PA system, and through the smoke and dust I tried to direct people to the emergency exits. One guy who had obviously had a few too many, stupidly came up to me, quick with his insults. "You think you're wonderful with your microphone," he said, but he had no idea what had just happened because of his consumption of alcohol.

Unsure how to control the people and get them out quickly, Eddie began shouting. "Quick, quick, play the fire tune, play the fire tune," he yelled. We had never rehearsed *Three Blind Mice,* our saxophone player, the ultimate in his music profession, piped up. "What key do you want me to play it in?" he asked. Utterly speechless, there was a short pause, followed by many expletives, and finally, "Just ***** play it!" It's crazy isn't it, in the midst of death, destruction and frenzy, *Three Blind Mice* rang out. The staff went to their positions and people were escorted off the premises, mainly though the back doors. Little did we know then that *Three Blind Mice* saved nearly three hundred lives.

I was aware that within minutes, the television stations would announce that any keyholders in the Abercorn area should return to their premises, as was the norm. I knew that Hilary would see this and be obviously concerned. I tried to go with the crowd, but as I turned into the foyer, the floor was missing. I balanced on the beams to get to the public telephone. Sadly, it was a sight that will never leave my mind. When I looked down there was carnage. Bodies were lying on the ground floor with limbs missing, as fire crews tried to rescue them. As I balanced on a floor beam, I managed to get a call through to Hilary and then I carried Max, who was a cot-case, in my arms, and escaped the building. I found out that my friend Trevor Kelly had been almost blown down the stairs, but he was okay. As I emerged out of the dust, the first thing that was thrust into my face was a television camera. "What's it like in there?" a reporter asked. My blood boiled over and before I knew it, I had pushed him out of the way.

When we got Max out, his legs were like jelly. "That's it, I'm on the next plane home," he said. It took us a long time to coax him back; he had been wonderful. But that was a pivotal point when we decided that as Clubsound, enough was enough.

Abercorn restaurant bomb, March 4, 1972. Two young women were murdered and 130 injured. A child being rescued with her bloodied mother following behind.

Vigilante groups were soon formed in the two waring communities, Protestant and Catholic. These groups created no-go areas and where we lived was no exception. Before long, it was our front door that got knocked on one night. One was not asked, one was told, "Your turn to man the barricades."

Hilary got word to me while I was away playing that the petrol station directly behind our home had been smashed. The street lights had been cut down and put across the roads to create barricades. As she watched, she expected a spark to come out of the electric lights which would cause the petrol station to explode, but thanks be to God, this never happened.

After being reluctantly recruited as a vigilante, and following the bomb at the Abercorn, and the near explosive petrol station behind our home, we decided that it was time to leave Belfast.

We had been the resident band in the Abercorn from 1970 to 1972, and agents coming to the club were always coaxing us to go to England as an act. They thought that our band could make it and we were better than most of the bands who were being brought in. We said no at first because Tommy, the drummer, didn't want to travel. Then the agent said, "I can get you work in South Africa; there's a whole new world opening up out there with British acts." I thought about it and agreed with the rest of the band that this could be a new start for us and our families, and an escape from the Troubles. Sadly, Tommy didn't want to go, so we found Davy McKnight, who had been with the Freshman showband and we became a six-piece band, instead of a five-piece band. Eddie McCrudden, one of the keyboard player's, asked his son Barry to join us on the saxophone. We rehearsed for a long time and became an excellent tight band.

It was the beginning of 1972, but as it turned out, we couldn't get the contract in South Africa until the beginning of 1973. So, we had a year's wait as there was already a band performing in Claridge's Hotel in Durban, which was our destination. The agent who had approached us about South Africa, said, "Look, if you really want to get out of Northern Ireland, before South Africa, then we can arrange for you to play in England." So, Hilary and I rented a place in between Oldham and Rochdale, called Royton, and we had a wee house there. During this time, Hilary was carrying our first child. When the time came for our baby to be born, we moved back to Belfast. Our son, Jason, was born on July 1, 1972. Soon after, I moved back to England to work and Hilary moved in with her parents.

Regrettably, I didn't see my son Jason, grow up in his first year. I should have been there to see him, but I wasn't. In those days, for most of the week I was performing and playing. And for the majority of the time, I was performing in England. So, I missed out on watching him grow for the first year and a half of his life.

In just one year, in the run up to our move to South Africa, we became one of the biggest names in the cabaret circuits in the North of England, and we changed our name from Clubsound to Warm Sensation. We finished up playing in the same clubs as Dame Shirley Bassey, Gene Pitney and Tony Christie. We were based in Manchester, but we also travelled to Newcastle in the north-east and as far afield as Wales and Birmingham. The cabaret six-piece band was not a well-paid job, therefore we tried to make more money by playing up to two or three spots a night, for six nights a week. The demand for us was exceptional and one of the big variety clubs, in Batley, named us as their nomination for *club act* of the year. We were literally at the top of our tree in the cabaret club circuit. The agent begged us to stay in England by saying that we would have been able to get on television, but unfortunately our contract was about to start in South Africa.

One of the last shows, which we played before we came home, was at the Wookey Hollow in Liverpool. We didn't get paid very much in those days and we had to work really hard for seven nights a week, often doing what we called doubles and triples each night. I had accumulated about a hundred pounds to bring home. I had saved this from my earnings. Somehow I lost the money and panicked. Whether it was taken from my dressing room or during my trips in and out of the building, bringing in the equipment, I don't know. I had intended to bring this money home in time for Christmas. And it was gone and my heart was broken. It was shocking. I was so annoyed, but when I got home, Hilary was very understanding and all was forgiven. People were inclined to think that we were living a glamourous life, but the reality was, it was hard earnt money.

At Christmas time in 1973, we returned home to Northern Ireland and had a wonderful time together with the family. My father offered to take us to the airport after Christmas for the long-haul flight to South Africa. As I mentioned earlier, my father who never showed affection, yet at the airport he said, "Take care of yourself son, and I'll see you when you come home."

CHAPTER 6

South Africa Calls

Warm Sensation was all set to go to South Africa and we were very excited. When we arrived, we had little knowledge about the area or what we would find once we got there. We went straight to the hotel where we would be performing the shows and also where we would be staying. It was a very posh hotel similar to The Savoy in London. Inside Claridge's Hotel there was the club where we would be playing. It was on the second floor and it was called The Cat's Whiskers. We loved the grandeur of the hotel, but we were living very tightly knit together in adjacent rooms, because all the guys had brought their wives. The wives were friendly, but if one didn't get on with another, it spread dissent among the camp, so to speak. It became claustrophobic because we were working for six nights every week while at the weekend we were playing matinées. This meant that our only day off each week was a Sunday. In the end, we were living in the corridor of the hotel. We were literally living in each other's pockets every day, meeting up and having breakfast together, and going through the same motions. It was like being back in Germany again, only plusher and more luxurious. The hotel was close to a beautiful beach, so when we could, we visited the beach or went shopping. Outside of that though, we were more or less pinned to the hotel. We made friends with the South Africans and they took us away for a day on a Sunday, as that was our only chance for a break away from the hotel.

We soon became aware that apartheid was well established. It suddenly dawned on us that we had left one battlefield to go into another, which was not quite the fresh start that we had hoped.

During the apartheid era, there was a kind of pecking order. There seemed to be three stages — Whites, Asians and the Bantus (Natives). The Asians were allowed to work in the bars and sell the drinks, but the Bantus were only allowed to work in the kitchens and had to be kept out of sight. They worked extremely long hours and were picked up at their settlements, outside Durban in their villages, and they were brought in to work by coach. They were picked up at four in the morning to begin work at six, and they worked through until seven or eight at night. I was horrified to discover that some of the Bantus who lived too far away, were living on the roof of this luxury hotel in makeshift huts. Opposite the hotel, there were beautiful parks with large signs which said, WHITE CHILDREN ONLY. At Durban Bay, sharks were common, but in the bay, where only whites were allowed, they had a shark net to keep them out. At the other two bays further up the coast, which were for non-whites, there were no shark nets.

The worst incident I witnessed was white ambulances and black ambulances. Hard as it is to believe now, they had white ambulances for white people and black ambulances for black people. If a white person had an accident, they waited for a white ambulance. But if a black ambulance came along, it would stop for the white person. On the other hand, if a black person had an accident and a white ambulance came by, then it drove on, and the black person had to wait for a black ambulance, even if they were dying. The black police patrolled in both black and white areas, but they had sticks instead of guns; while the white police had plenty of guns.

One day Hilary and I were walking through a lovely park, when two black policemen came over to us. "Can you come with us?" one of them asked. Knowing the risks that are involved in South Africa, I asked them why. "Could you please come with us to the other side of the

park?" was the reply. We followed them, and near another entrance to
the park lay a white man in the middle of the flower bed; he was drunk
and had fallen asleep. This was a regular occurrence as huge numbers
of Afrikaners regularly came to Durban from their farming areas and
spent the weekend drinking. Unfortunately, Durban was renowned
for attracting heavy drinkers and the Afrikaners often picked fights
with black people for no reason. "Could you please give him a shake
and wake him? We aren't allowed to touch him," one of them said.
Naturally, I obliged and once he woke, they told him to move on.

George and Hilary in South Africa, 1973.

We had only been in South Africa a short while, when our wee son, aged
only one and a half years old, became seriously ill. His body went limp,
his little face turned blue and he had an extremely high temperature. It
frightened us both. We were absolutely panic-stricken, so we rang hotel
reception. They rang a doctor immediately and one came straightaway.
I believe that God sent that doctor, because without him, we would
have lost our child. When the doctor arrived, he stripped Jason and
immersed him in a bath of cold water. Then he called an ambulance
which rushed him to Addington Hospital, which was renowned for
successful heart surgery, and it was also where the famous Doctor
Christiaan Barnard, who performed the world's first human-to-human

heart transplant, operated. As soon as he arrived, the doctor placed our son onto ice, beside a fan to get his temperature down. After tests, we were given three possible prognosis's — typhoid, malaria or meningitis. By that time, we were terrified. We were in South Africa, a long way from home, and had only been there a month or so. We will always remember Doctor Baize, who literally took Jason under his wing. Then the final result came through — it was typhoid. Jason remained on a critical list for about four weeks because they were terrified that it would get into his blood. They were trying to stop it before it went into his bowel region. If it had, he would have died because it would have been impossible to save him.

For six weeks he was in intensive care, which really concerned us. Sometimes when we visited, we were not allowed to go in and see him as he was in isolation, so we would only be able to look at him through a window. He had lost so much weight and become incredibly thin. Hilary ended up on Valium, and her weight reduced to six stone. Every day, she walked up and down the beach and prayed. This was a time that we had turned to God unexpectedly. Hilary prayed and I prayed to this God, who I knew existed, that my mother had told me about, and I needed him. After about six weeks, Jason was allowed to leave the hospital. Hilary began feeding him because we believed he'd caught the typhoid from an infected fly that landed on his ice-cream. Hilary cooked every single meal for him on a Primus stove in the hotel room until he got his strength back. We told the hotel that we were going to do this because Hilary wouldn't feed him outside of the hotel and she wouldn't let him out of the hotel either. I decided when Jason regained his strength, that Hilary should take him home as soon as she could. He needed to be back in a healthier climate as his immunity had fallen and he was very weak. When Hilary began to pack, she found all his baby clothes and considered giving them away.

Each of the floors in the hotel, had a servant and we had got to know the servant on our floor. Knowing that she had a young baby, Hilary gave her the baby clothes and never thought anymore about it. Whether the maid had said something or someone had seen and reported her, she was called into the office and fired from her position because she had accepted a gift from white people. Soon after, I was called into the manager's office. "Do you realise what you have done? Your wife gave clothes to a Black native," the Dutch manager said. "So what?" I replied, but his next response was arrogant. "That is against the law here." My blood started to boil because of all the wrongs I had seen. "Well let me tell you, I come from Northern Ireland and this is not normal. If my wife wants to look after another woman's child by giving her clothes for the child, she'll do it whether you like it or not. What can you do about it?" I replied. His response was swift. "You can be fired." We were like two bulls with locked horns. "Why don't you fire us then?!" I replied. I knew with the band being so popular, he would have to answer to his bosses as to why he had fired us. I was determined to show him that it's okay to be kind.

As soon as Jason was well enough, I sent him home with my wife. In those days, it took five flights to get there. Hilary had to fly via such places as Kenya, Switzerland and London, which she had to do on her own. She was absolutely exhausted and unfortunately, Jason was teething, so it was a difficult journey. When she arrived in Belfast, she moved back in with her parents. But the good news was that our son became healthy again.

Meanwhile, I had decided to stay on and work the rest of my contract with the boys, until the end of the year. I suddenly realised that this was not the utopia that we had hoped it would be. So, I made up my mind that I was coming home at the end of the year until events determined otherwise. About a month later, my sister phoned me with the dreaded words that I did not want to hear. "Dad has cancer, he is very ill and it does not look like he's going to come through." My only option, I believed, was to return home. However, Dad had told her to tell me not to. But I had to go; my decision was made. I informed the boys in the band that I was heading home. They were sympathetic yet still upset as my departure would create such a hole in the band. As I was still under contract to South Africa, and the head of the hotel brought me in and went through all my finances. He was determined not to let me go. In fact, I thought that he was going to stop me from getting on the plane. He deducted the cost of the hotel, food and flights etcetera because I had breached my contract. I still had to pay for the hospital bills and flights and I only just managed to scrape the money together. Thankfully, my footballer friends, who played for Arsenal, helped by driving me to the airport. I was so grateful to them as they didn't have to do that, which when I reflect, I believe was God blessing me. With their help, I began my long journey home on five flights. I arrived in Belfast an hour before the funeral, but not in time to see my beloved Dad. They had closed the coffin and wouldn't let me open it. He was a big man, and apparently he'd shrunk once the cancer spread. We carried him from his home and buried him in Roselawn Cemetery in Belfast.

I have only had a few regrets in my life, thankfully, compared to most people. One of them was the decision to go to South Africa, where I nearly lost my beloved son and didn't have the chance to say goodbye to my beloved father. Being so far away from home deprived me of getting home in time to see him one last time, which is a sad regret.

George's Dad. He wouldn't have known if that was a banjo or a ukulele.

That was the end of South Africa for me. We had made an album there, but it was never released. We got a long weekend off and travelled to Johannesburg to record it; the recording was completed in three days. If I could only get my hands on those tapes; they were brilliant. It's very sad.

When I got home to Northern Ireland, it was like starting all over again. All I had left was one hundred and fifty pounds in my pocket and a guitar. My father had left me his little estate car, but that was it. We had nowhere to live, so I moved in with Hilary's parents, who were wonderful to us. When we originally left for South Africa, we had been in this beautiful house, which we had done up and rented for a pound a week, but unfortunately, we'd had to leave it.

I soon began playing music again to earn money and started up a three-piece band with Tommy Thomas, the original drummer of Clubsound, who wouldn't travel. At my father's graveside during the burial, I saw a family friend called Joe Gibson, who was a sales manager at the Goblin Vacuum Cleaning Company near where I lived. He kindly offered me a job. So, I began working straightaway, with twenty men and four hundred women. All I had to do was turn the metal sections over on a lathe, but I was tearing my hair out with boredom. All the girls and guys recognised me from the Abercorn cabaret club days. They used to come up to me and want my autograph, and say things such as, "Why are you working here?" This really embarrassed me, as I was a respected figure in show business and had been reduced to working on a lathe. From that point on, I ate my lunch in the car because I couldn't cope with all the attention. I had no choice but to persevere with this job to earn money for my family. On the outside, it looked as if I was pulling my life back together with a new job, but on the inside, it was tearing me apart because I had to work my way up again.

CHAPTER 7

Health versus Wealth

During this period, I was walking through Belfast one day with Hilary, when I bumped into a man called George Mullan, who I'd known for years. George had played with a band called Witnesses in the showband years and he had become the general sales manager of Smyths for Records, a chain of eight to ten record stores. They had record shops in nearly every town in Northern Ireland. They also sold record players, radios and general electrical goods. George became a great friend and was good to me; I owe a lot to him. Once again, I wonder now if he was sent to me by God. He said that he didn't know that I was home from South Africa and asked me where I was working and where I was living. I told him that I was working on a lathe at the Goblin Vacuum Cleaning Company and I was living with my wife's parents. "No, you're not," he replied. "You don't have to work there," he added. The following week, he had me working in one of Smyths' shops on Church Lane beside the Abercorn. This was great as it boosted my wages and I was able to get a mortgage for a new home. It was a gorgeous semi-detached house at 134 Barnetts Road, in the Stormont area. It had a lovely little garden at the front and the back. Billy, my brother-in-law and I redesigned the house inside. Soon after we moved in, Hilary became pregnant with our second child. It turned out to be a place where we would spend many happy years.

George Mullan was insistent that I progress with Smyths for Records. "We're bringing in a new hi-fi range called Dynatron. You know a lot about music, can you wire up a showroom for me?" he said one day. Of course, I said, yes. Soon, a beautiful range of period walnut furniture arrived, with hi-fi's set in them. Instead of wiring them up separately, I wired them all up so that they were linked together. When customers walked in, they were able to view the whole range. At the flick of a button, I could switch from one to the next to let them hear each one. A position then became available in one of Smyths shops at Donegal Place in Belfast, for an assistant manager. I got the job and then about six months later they made me a full-time manager, in Bangor. We were one of the biggest branches on the circuit. In the mid-seventies, colour televisions were becoming popular. Everybody wanted one and Smyths decided to bring in the full range; I was selling them like sweets. Unsurprisingly, as we were one of the biggest stores, our sales figures went through the roof. Our customers didn't even want us to unpack them; they were that desperate to get their hands on one. Suppliers were bringing them in the lorry loads, such was the demand. It was like another God-send for me because it made our branch in Bangor, one of the most successful.

On September 25, 1974, our daughter Natalie was born; she was a beautiful baby. But when she was about six weeks old, I thought that something wasn't quite right. We noticed how other babies tried to interact with you, but Natalie was vacant. I waved my hand in front of her face, but I didn't want to alarm Hilary, so I got a lighter and waved it before her eyes, but she never followed it. At first, I thought maybe she was just a slow developer with her eyesight. I told Hilary, but instead of going to the doctor, she went to the clinic. The nurse examined her and with no consideration or feeling, she just turned round quite abruptly and said, "I'm sorry Mrs Jones, but no, she can't see." My wife nearly fainted. Hilary phoned me at work in the office with the news, and we just couldn't believe it. We had only recently recovered from nearly losing Jason and we had hit rock bottom with our finances again. Talk about a terrible two to three years; we were dumbfounded.

Heroically, my sister came to the rescue as though she had been assigned by God, yet again. Natalie had congenital cataracts. They assumed that it was from the forceps' birth, but we were unable to point the finger. The damage was done, and she'd been badly bruised when she was born. Anyway, we had heard on the grapevine that there was this man who was really advanced in eyesight issues; he had invented equipment to look behind the eye. This was a long time before anyone had heard of lasers. His name was Professor Eric Cowan. As I've mentioned, we were just getting on our feet and had bought a semi-detached house for £4,500. We didn't know who to turn to for help in those days. We knew that money would have opened doors, but we didn't have that option. On hearing this, my sister, Lally, was both perturbed and annoyed. "This guy could do something for you?" she said. "Yes," I replied and told her his name. "I remember that name," she replied. My sister never threw anything out; she kept every little piece of paper. She was the one who had completed the research about Cromwell and our ancestors, which I mentioned earlier. This was a chance in a million that Lally had remembered this professor's name. We were literally distraught and didn't know who to turn to. This answer to the prayer in our hearts can only have come from God. Her husband, my late brother-in-law, was a master bookbinder. Highly trained, he could do anything with books, including binding them in leather or gilding them in gold. "I'm sure that Billy bound a thesis for Eric Cowan. I remember the name," she said. Lally kept every letter. She searched through her files and found a letter, thanking Billy for his amazing work. She rang Eric Cowan and lo and behold, we got our child in two days later. And there was Lally, saving our lives again. Professor Cowan told us that there was good news and bad news. "The bad news is that she cannot see, but the good news is that if I can get light into the back of her eyes before the muscles deteriorate, then she might have a little sight, but only partial. If I don't get light into the back of her eyes very soon, then she will be completely blind." Even before lasers, they used to take out the cataract with a wee sucker and it was a miniature operation. But in our day, he had to cut her lenses to try

and get the cataract out. What happens is that the cataract shatters
into micro pieces, so subsequently her lenses had been damaged and
disfigured. But it was worth it, to get light into the back of her eye.
Then Natalie went for another six operations to remove the bits that
were floating around. As a result, at the age of one or two, she had to
wear contact lenses. Then to give her eyes a rest, she had little glasses
with an elastic round the back of her head.

That child has been through what you wouldn't believe. But with God's
help, by taking her to Professor Cowan; a fraction of her sight was saved.

Whereas some children might have fully depended on their parents
and given in to life's challenges, in Natalie's case with her partial sight,
we always encouraged Natalie to try new things, not that we thought
of her as any different to other children.

Her heroism and bravery came from God, I believe, and she even tried
water skiing and snow skiing. When we taught her water skiing, she
learnt by holding onto a rope at the back of the boat that she couldn't
see. When Hilary was driving the boat, I had to lean out of the back and
shout through a megaphone that we were turning left or turning right.
She was literally doing it blind with a rope. She took to it amazingly
well, but that didn't seem to be enough for Natalie, as we found out.
She wanted to progress with her water skiing even more. She always
seemed to have a sense of wanting to prove to herself and to everyone
else that her sight wasn't going to hold her back.

One summer, when she was quite young, we spent a week at the lakes
in Enniskillen, water skiing. At that point, Natalie had just learnt how
to water ski on two skis. We had to go home at the end of the week,
but the family who we shared the caravan park with, who we knew
very well, told us to leave Natalie there. They would take care of her
and she could play with their kids. We thought about it and agreed.
We talked Natalie through everything that she would need to do, and
gave instructions to the family not to leave her anywhere because of
her eyes. They were wonderful Christian people, so we knew that she'd

be alright. We went home on the Wednesday of that week as I had some business to attend to, and planned to return on the Saturday. The amazing thing was, that when we returned, the father of the family had taught Natalie to ski on just one water ski — a mono ski. But Natalie wasn't satisfied with that; when we arrived, she was being pulled behind the boat, to our amazement, on a disc with a chair on it. That was the sort of inspiration that fired us on to encourage her in every way.

Nothing seemed to be a challenge for Natalie, so we decided at the age of seven or eight to take her snow skiing. Within three days, she had learnt how to ski on the slopes, and as long as she could see her mum's coloured anorak in front of her, she skied perfectly.

It's hard to believe, but at the age of about eleven, Natalie began being bullied at school. We were angry about the whole thing, and sometimes blamed ourselves. This happened because at primary school, she had a classroom assistant who looked after her and a principal who realised how hard it was for Natalie to attain levels because of her disability. Despite her challenges, she progressed incredibly well at Kilmaine Primary School, so much so, that in her final year, she was awarded the Principal's Prize. We then had to make a decision about which school Natalie was going to move on to. She sat a transfer assessment which was under the auspices of the Eleven Plus to test her ability because her partial sight, which she passed with flying colours. However, Hilary and I had reservations about sending Natalie to a grammar school as we knew that the academic standards would be higher. We didn't want her to be under any pressure because of the limitations of her eyesight. In addition to that, there were many children who were leaving Natalie's primary school at the same time and moving on to the comprehensive high school. Taking all that into consideration, we decided not to send Natalie to the grammar school, but sent her instead to Bangor Girls' High School. We thought that the children from primary school would help her in the corridors and down the stairs, but sadly, that was not the case. As I said earlier, we blamed ourselves because we felt that we had made the wrong decision, because she was bullied at the high school. It was a terrible time for Natalie; the children used to take her Walkman and put it on the top of one of the cupboards in the classroom where she wouldn't be able to find it. Another disastrous time was when the school decided to go on a skiing trip. By this time, Natalie had progressed to a good standard of skiing. Nonetheless, we still expressed our concerns to the teachers, who assured us that she would be fine. Hilary made sure that her teachers knew that Natalie's skiing ability depended on others being with her. We're not sure how this happened, but Natalie was taken high up to the top of the slope. The girls who accompanied her then took off Natalie's glasses. At this point, Natalie wore thick *bottle-end* glasses and I'm sure you can only imagine how distraught she was. Although she normally wore contact lenses, she was unable to wear them when she went skiing. After these girls left Natalie stranded, thankfully, a ski instructor arrived and took her down safely.

When Hilary and I eventually found out, we were horrified and very angry. We approached the principal, who knew who the perpetrators were, and demanded that he do something about it. When it became clear, that he wasn't going to do anything, it prompted Hilary and I to make an informed decision. One of the things that had helped Natalie through her difficult time was horse riding. "Why don't we move away from Bangor and get a small cottage out in the countryside, where Natalie would be able to do some more riding," I said to Hilary. This was a decision that we had to make for Natalie's welfare, as it was clear that nothing was going to change for her at Bangor High school. We thought that if we moved out of the area, we could find another school that would look after her. We bought a little cottage in Mountstewart Road, Newtownards, in 1988; which was beside a huge National Trust property. We lived on the road that runs alongside the estate wall. At that time, Hilary had gradually been introducing Natalie to horse riding. She rode ponies at a nearby riding school. We discovered that if we got something for Natalie to concentrate on, it would take her mind off the bullying. Hilary and I decided that horse riding would be the perfect activity to occupy her.

Having already committed to buying the house, we investigated local schools. We had heard that Regent House in Newtownards had a high academic standard. In addition, it was a mixed school, which we thought would be better for Natalie. I approached the principal, Mr Orr, and told him about the bullying that Natalie had suffered at her previous school. It turned out that Mr Orr knew me from radio which made us all feel at ease. He assured us that he would get Natalie a classroom assistant to look after her and that she would be made very welcome. We were happy that Natalie was now moving from a comprehensive high school into a grammar school, which Hilary and I thought that we should have done in the first place. In her new school, Natalie blossomed; there was no bullying and as a result, Natalie's progress soared.

Unbeknown to us, when we bought this cottage, there was a woman further down the road, called Sheila Wilson, who had beautiful stables. We went down and explained the situation and Sheila opened her arms to Natalie after hearing about the bullying stories and realising her disability. She asked Natalie to work in the stables with her and Natalie's love for horses grew and grew. We found out that this was the answer to take her mind off the hurt that the bullying had caused. The horse riding then became another challenge for Natalie to overcome so we decided to buy her a pony. We gave it to her as a surprise in Sheila Wilson's stables. From that moment on, Natalie began her progression to top level dressage, which takes a number of years to complete. Her desire was to compete in the paralympic games. However, we were totally baffled when we were told by the paralympic committee, that Natalie's eyesight was just one per cent too good to let her on to the team. The Irish team desperately wanted Natalie because she had won every award on her beloved horse, Magnum, which proved that she was an expert in competing at a high level in show jumping. When it came to cross-country, Natalie and her mum would walk the whole cross-country course on the morning of the competition. Then Natalie would climb onto Magnum and do it from memory. Our hearts were in our mouths as we left her at the starting point because we were not allowed to accompany her on any part of the cross-country course. However, her horse Magnum, sensed the fact that Natalie needed his help and if Natalie was guiding the horse in a slightly wrong direction, unable to predict where the gate was, then Magnum corrected and took her over the jump; it was absolutely incredible to watch. Natalie believed in the Lord so faithfully that we realised that this was the Lord touching her and our family. Little did we know at that stage that Natalie's love for the Lord and Christianity was to help us later on in life.

After that, nothing seemed to be a barrier for Natalie; it absolutely astounded us. She showed us the way and taught us how a disability should be managed. With her eyesight problem, she had been reduced to what was called six-nine metre vision with other complications. But despite her impairment, she progressed in all her A Levels and went on to study at Stranmillis University College, to pursue her desire to become a teacher. We felt it was going to be a massive challenge for her, but at the same time, didn't want her to be disappointed. Yet all we could do was encourage her and help her along the way. She studied every night at home with a magnified screen that fitted as a flip-top over the computer screen. When she was working with her books, it always had to be within six inches of her eyes so she could read, even with contact lenses which she wore from a very early age. With God's help, she made it.

Natalie progressed and went on to become a junior teacher and then a full-time teacher. Her first love was to teach special needs children and she soon obtained a position at Londonderry Primary School, in Newtownards. She then progressed to become head of the Special Needs Department, where she is still working today as a teacher.

* * *

Jason had left school with no academic prowess, in other words with no GCSEs or A Levels, and I thought that it was the time for him to progress into employment. Through a friend, I got him a job with a big shipping company called TR Shipping, which he rather enjoyed. The CEO, Tommy Rogers, was a great man and did a lot for Northern Ireland, but sadly he is no longer with us.

My son struck me as having similar character traits to me, so I said to him, "Do you know, I think that you would be great as a salesman because you definitely have the *gift of the gab.*" He took my advice and started working in Dixons which was a huge television and electrical store. He progressed well as a salesman and became an assistant manager in one of their branches. It was during this period that girls began to come along, and maybe I'm biased, but he's a bit of a good-looking boy. Therefore, girls were not a problem.

He progressed from being a salesman and decided for some particular reason, that he wanted to take up a trade. So, I introduced him to a friend, by the name of Eddie Hall, who was a master joiner, and Jason started learning carpentry. He spent one year doing an apprenticeship, but Jason, being like a chip off the old block, had itchy feet and wanted to see the world.

He and his friend, who were in their late teenage years, decided to get a train ticket that enabled them to travel around Europe; it had a special rate for students. He and his friend took a tent, and disappeared for about two months; continuously checking in at home I have to add. When he came back, I noticed that Jason had a permanent smile on his face because he had been introduced to the world of travel. It was then that Jason knew what he wanted to do. His first girlfriend came along. Her name was Elizabeth, and we were pleased. Then out of the blue, they decided that they wanted to spend a year visiting Australia.

By then, Jason, was in his twenties and had the responsibility of looking after his girlfriend. They checked in at regular intervals and sent us photographs. Jason, with his natural chatter, secured jobs in Irish pubs. He worked as a barman, bearing in mind that he'd had no training. But because he had an infectious smile, the Aussie's loved him and they were always given jobs in Irish pubs as they travelled around.

After ten months, their year of travelling was coming to an end. Jason rang and said that one night he had got down on one knee and proposed to Elizabeth. Hilary and I thought, wow, this is it; the start of our family. They came home and bought a house near the village where we lived. They were married in Newtownards. It was an incredible day, and we thought it was wonderful that our family was enlarging and that they lived so close. They had also secured great jobs; Jason applied for a job at NTL, which was a communications and information technology network in Belfast. Meanwhile, Elizabeth applied for a job in banking and she too was successful. Jason flourished in his position and we were relieved that he had now found his niche.

Sadly, after only one year, Jason openly admitted that the marriage wasn't working and they parted company amicably. A short while later, Jason built his own house in a place called Ballywalter, which is close to our home. It was a beautiful house that Jason and his mother designed.

* * *

Meanwhile, I had hooked up with Tommy Thomas and we began playing again in our spare time. My love of the music scene was rekindled and our three piece became five, and we decided to change the band's name back to Clubsound. I had begun to earn good money so once again, I left my manager's position at the shop, to go full-time with my band once more. Was it another mistake again, perhaps?

The original three guys were me, Tommy and Crawford Bell, a well-known country singer and trumpet player, but we needed a guitar player, so we drafted in Alan McCartney. He was a great guitarist who was well known and had been with the Plattermen. However, we were still looking for a keyboard player. One day, when I was working in Smyths for Records, which also sold electronic organs, by chance, Barry Woods, who I knew was a great musician from the past, walked into the shop. "Where are you working now?" I asked him. He said that he was playing with a band called Tweed, down in Kilkenny, but he had to travel back to Bangor where he lived. "We're looking for a keyboard player in our band and I could also get you a job in this shop, demonstrating keyboards and organs. Would you be interested?" I said. "That would be terrific," he replied. Then we were five.

Our original guitar player, Billy Bingham, who had been in the original Clubsound and in South Africa with us, had decided to come home. Crawford Bell wanted to concentrate on his studio work, so he left the band. Billy re-joined us and that's how we became a five-piece band again under the name of Clubsound. After many rehearsals, we decided that we should go to golf clubs and social clubs to perform.

Then late in 1974, a local booking agent, Joe Davies, approached us to say that a residency had become available at the Railway Bar in Antrim. It was owned by a chap called Joe Mullholland. We would be able to perform as a resident band on Thursday, Friday and Saturday nights.

Clubsound in the Railway Bar in Antrim, 1974.

Tommy, our original drummer, was also a songwriter. He was a Welsh guy, who had come over with the armed forces before the Troubles.

When he'd been in the army he met a girl from Omagh, County Tyrone and they'd got married and settled in Northern Ireland. He had spent his life in military bands and proved to be a great jazz drummer and drum teacher. He was a funny and gifted man, and when he began writing comedy sketches and parodies, he showed them to me, and I would tell him how to say things in a Northern Ireland style. We became a writing duo and it was all Northern Irish humour. He was a great scriptwriter and comedian, who produced hilarious material. At that time, one of the most loved of Northern Ireland's comedians, James Young, passed away. So, we were more or less carrying on his mantle. This was also the time when we changed from just playing music to becoming a comedy showband with cabaret. Doing impressions came naturally to me. As I mentioned earlier, my sister used to let me perform on the telephone system for the other operators at her workplace. When I was the MC in the band, I started to heckle while Tommy began acting comically behind me. A comedy band was born and I became the characters that he was creating. We then began to write what became one of our most famous singles.

You might remember that years ago people used to come round with suitcases. They were called travelling salesmen and they sold all sorts of things. Tommy created this character from India who sold ladies' underwear, but he didn't realise that he was walking into a different religious area, and he was totally unaware of what was going on in Northern Ireland. It became a classic anthem, which we called *Belfast Belfast*. Owing to political correctness, we are unable to present it like we used to. However, people still laugh at it to this very day.

We also needed a B side, which was about the British Army, and the trouble they had trying to understand our accents in Northern Ireland. It was called *The Professionals* and it was about how we say things differently, and how we educated the British soldiers. Even though we were speaking English, they couldn't understand us. I played a character who said in an Irish accent, "I'm now going til (tell) you how to speak Ulster — I'm going to knock your melt in." Then the officer who was acting as a British Interpreter would say, "He's going to biff you severely," in a traditional English accent. Then there was:

"He's like a herrin' with the back out of him, that means, he's a very thin fellow."

"She's like the back end of a bus, she's a very fat lady."

"Here's a wee drop in your hand, I will give you a cup of tea."

I was the perfect fall guy for Tommy and his ideas. He was very funny when he dressed up as well. This provided humour that was a light relief. We also took the mickey out of famous politicians. We imitated their accents and mannerisms so well that people thought that they were actually in the room. Yet, we never put anyone down, and never took any sides, we were always very careful, because one night we could be playing in a Protestant hall, the following night in a Catholic hall, so everything had to be tasteful humour with some thought behind it. And unlike today, we never used expletives in our comedy, nor did we find it necessary to do so.

So, after thinking that we were going to play in a bar, we ended up at this residency for three and a half years, and it turned out to be one of the most popular venues for entertainment in Northern Ireland.

People needed somewhere to go to escape, have a laugh and enjoy the music. So, people started travelling from all over to see us and that's what elevated the band. Catholics and Protestants mingled together and they didn't seem to mind if they were sitting next to each other. If you didn't get to the car park by six o'clock on a Saturday evening, then that was it, you didn't get in; the queues were that long. Amazingly, the people travelled from all over to Antrim. They certainly seemed to be enjoying themselves and by the end of the night they often staggered out of the bar.

We weren't aware how well known we were becoming. But it wasn't long before we recorded our first album called Clubsound Capers, in 1975, with the songs, *Belfast Belfast* and *Shankill Airways*. It sold upwards of 40,000. Because of the success of its sales, we received a genuine authorised silver disc from the British Phonographic Industry (BPI) organisation. By today's standards, the album would have gone five times platinum because it sold all over the world to Irish expats.

Silver disc — Clubsound Capers.

One of our biggest fans was Lord Peter Melchett, a junior minister in the House of Lords. During a number of our shows, he slipped into the back of the hall with his bodyguards, and clearly enjoyed the night. He had perceived how much work we were doing to bring people together, and it was an honour when he presented us with our first silver disc at dinner. Soon after, he gave a speech in the House of Lords about us and the work we were doing to help people come together.

During the Railway Bar years in Antrim, the owner Joe Mullholland, was what I would call a herder. He kept herding people into his bar like cattle; often over three times the number who should have been allowed in. Packed in tightly with everyone sweating, it was a problem when someone needed the toilet, as nearly everyone had to move. It became such an issue that on occasions we had to stop playing to move out of their way.

I remember one night when I had to stop playing at least three times, until I got fed up. When the next person came, I jumped off the stage and followed them to the toilets with my guitar. That night no one went to the toilets after that. "I wonder what they went into that room for?" I shouted as I jumped back on to the stage. But everyone laughed it off, as they were having such a good time. On another occasion, when a group of women got up to go to the toilet, I singled them out. "I've just given this song a big build-up; it's going to be wonderful and now you're going to miss it by going to the toilet," I said. I think we became famous for that act because we stopped people from going to the toilet. When people used to invite their friends to come and see Clubsound, they would say, "Now for goodness' sake, don't get up to go to the toilet in the middle of their songs, or they will follow you."

As the band became more well-known we played in bigger venues, yet sadly the Troubles seemed to be getting worse. After what we had witnessed in our shows with Protestants and Catholics coming together and singing, we thought it would be lovely to record a peace anthem. It was called *Peace, The Time is Now.*

Peace the Time is Now

(Chorus)

The time is here, the time is now,

the time for all mankind,

to join together hands for peace,

and leave all wars behind.

We decided to do this song at the end of each night and what astounded us was as soon as we started playing this song, people stood up and linked arms and sang it with us. These were the people who were showing their distaste for the Troubles of any sort in their own country and we felt that we had also achieved something else by doing this. That song was only one of two. After the popularity of the peace song, we re-recorded the old Abba song, *The Way Old Friends Do,* and it got exactly the same reaction at the end of the night. It was like *Auld Lang Syne* that is sung on New Year's Eve. The audience might have been sitting together in close proximity and not known each other, but while we were singing this song, they became instant friends, irrespective of their religion or beliefs. We felt very proud during our Clubsound years that this was one of the things that we'd achieved. I wondered if this was God working in me again by suggesting these songs.

The Way Old Friends Do

Times of joy and times of sorrow
We will always see it through
Oh, I don't care what comes tomorrow
We can face it together
The way old friends do

You and I can share the silence
Finding comfort together
The way old friends do

And after fights and words of violence
We make up with each other
The way old friends do
We can face it together
The way old friends do

These two songs became anthems of hope for those in attendance; not many had a dry eye in the house. If you lived in Northern Ireland at that time, or remember the atrocities that occurred, you will be aware that many families lost loved ones to the bomb and the gun.

I continued playing with Clubsound as a resident band for three nights a week. A lot of the Downtown presenters enjoyed coming to the Railway Bar to hear us. As I mentioned earlier, Tommy never wanted to travel, which is why he didn't go to South Africa. This residency suited us, but the band was becoming so popular that people wanted us to play for them on different nights, therefore, Tommy agreed to only play on Sunday nights. One of the first bookings that we took, was to play at Shorts' Social Club in Belfast. One evening when we arrived at Shorts' security entrance, the Bouncer told us they hadn't ordered any furniture. We looked at each other in disbelief, and wondered what he was talking about. Then we realised that the lorry Joe Mullholland had lent us, had furniture written on the side of it. Professionals or what?

We were amazed to find that on our first night at the Shorts' Club, we drew eight hundred people. We had certainly moved on from the Railway Bar, that held two hundred and fifty packed in. We were just astounded at the number of people who had come to see us, and they were all shouting, "Sing *Belfast Belfast* and *Shankill Airways,* and *Andy McFadden and his funky five wee piece band.*" We had a wonderful night and the next day the phone didn't stop ringing. Some of the most popular venues in Northern Ireland wanted to book the band to play in their clubs, and that was just for a Sunday night. Our weekends we were fully booked; we played in Antrim from Thursday until Saturday and at Shorts and other venues on Sunday nights.

Large amounts of money were being offered to us to travel up the country. It suddenly made us think, were we doing the right thing by staying as a resident band? We decided that it was time to seriously decide where our future lay.

It was then that, Jack Rogers, God rest his soul, who owned the Edenmore Hotel in Whiteabbey, a few miles outside Belfast entered into our lives. He was a successful entrepreneur with several businesses, including discos. "You guys are too big to be playing in just a residency, you guys should be travelling around Ireland, Scotland and further afield," He said. "Jack, we've done all that and we've been to England," I replied. "You know, this is something really special that you have. I think that it's time for you to leave and I'm happy to manage you," he added in an unwavering voice. So, we left the residency, but once again Tommy refused to come with us and decided to leave the band. As I mentioned earlier, Tommy only wanted to be part of a resident band and didn't want to travel.

Jack put money up for a media pack that included posters, flyers, interviews and advertisements. Clubsound were ready to get back on the road with Alan McCartney on guitar, Barry Woods on keyboard, Billy Bingham on guitar, Davy McKnight on drums. He had returned from South Africa and re-joined us, and me on vocals and bass guitar. This became the new line-up of the Clubsound band, most of which remains the same today.

We performed in large venues, made albums and released records. We also imitated voices of cartoon characters for television advertisements, one of which was McEwan's Lager. They became famous later on as the Ballymoor Grouse Beaters. We travelled to London to record the voices and we put Northern Ireland terminology into the script. Clubsound became totally synonymous with the Ballymoor Grouse Beaters. The cartoon ads became so successful, that we recorded six different ones. In the end, the ads became more popular than the product because the product didn't live up to the ads. So we decided to make a record, and we brought out a track on one of our albums called, *The Ballymoor Grouse Beaters*.[5] So, that's how it emerged, from simply doing these ads, that the band became as popular as they were. We even had our own television series on BBC Northern Ireland and it was all because

---

5 Ballymoor Grouse Beaters link; https://www.youtube.com/watch?v=zIOzu4YVbu8

of Jack Rogers' guidance. He flew to Carnaby Street, in London, just to get us smart suits that were a little bit different. He had them made especially for us. "Where did you get those suits from?" people asked. He just wanted us to look really professional. His main goal was to get us to Las Vegas, but he took us to Scotland and England, and we played in all the top clubs there and with that we ended up landing a BBC television series. All during this, he was chasing a guy called Charles Mathers from Las Vegas who booked the acts at the MGM Grand. He had heard a lot about of us apparently, but he never came to see us.

Clubsound on their BBC television show.

We thought our chance had come for Charles Mathers to see us because we were offered a wonderful opportunity to play at Jolly's nightclub in Stoke-on-Trent. It was owned by a Jewish family and they had just been awarded the accolade of Club of the Year, so they were planning one of their biggest nights ever. People such as Lord Bernard Delfont, Lord Lew Grade and various other dignitaries were invited. Headlining that wonderful night was Ronnie Corbett. Paul Daniels, was the compere and Pans People, the dancers; Carl Wayne, who was formerly from The Move and a young bright protégé from the West End who had been discovered playing the part of Annie, in the famous musical. And not forgetting us — Clubsound. Very excited, we turned up at Jolly's nightclub which held about two thousand people, for rehearsals. The owners of the club insisted that everything was done perfectly because this was their biggest night ever. So, they brought in a film director called Max Butterfield to direct the entire show. The rehearsals started and Pans People went on and rehearsed their two sections. Then Carl Wayne went on and rehearsed his two songs. We were only allocated something like eleven or twelve minutes to try to cram in our act. But how do you encompass the highlights of Clubsound in eleven minutes? What were we going to do in that short time? How we were meant to encompass what we did into eleven minutes was nigh on impossible. We decided to do our tribute to the great Glenn Miller and also a feature that we had called *The Music Man,* which involved two of the guys playing six instruments on the one song. So, we stood up and performed *The Music Man* for the director and then we preceded to do our Glenn Miller tribute. He was absolutely ecstatic and everyone at rehearsals was impressed. Even Pans People were dancing at the back to the music. Max said we were wonderful and that he was going to promote us to second on the bill. And we were going to get an extra six minutes. So, we had seventeen minutes to prove ourselves. We rehearsed everything perfectly and we had to cut some parts out to make it fit into seventeen minutes. Everything was looking wonderful, the Rolls Royce's were pulling up, the women were looking beautiful in their dresses and all the dignitaries were arriving. Before they arrived, we walked around the tables and read the dignitaries' names on the name cards. And to our great surprise, there was a seat for Charles Mathers from the MGM Grand in Las Vegas. "This is your big chance guys," said Jack Rogers. At this point, we were really excited as everything was going brilliantly. We were in the dressing rooms; Pans People had gone on stage and then Little Annie went on. We felt calm and confident that we'd done enough rehearsals and we'd gauged it into our time schedule. We were ready. Messages were coming down from Lord Delfont, as Scotland and England were playing in the world cup. He wanted to know the results because we were watching television in the dressing rooms. And that made us feel even more relaxed. "Tell Lord Delfont what the score is," I said. Carl Wayne had just gone on stage and when he came back down. "Guys, they're a wonderful crowd. I heard you in rehearsals. You guys are going to storm it," he said. This gave us even more confidence. Paul Daniels was on stage doing some of his gags and getting ready to introduce the next act which was the one before us on the line-up. Then, all of a sudden, the intricate PA system cut out and stopped working. Panic set in and the Jewish family who were running it, dashed about tearing their hair out. Paul Daniels managed to find a battery-powered megaphone, so he was talking to two thousand people through this. "What are we gonna do? What are we gonna do?" said our guys as they rushed around. Then we remembered. "We've got our own PA in the bandwagon and we'd be happy to put it up for you if you can give us a moment.," I said to the Jewish family. "Please guys, do something," they replied. So, all the bouncers, the doormen and our roadies emptied the wagon and quickly put up our PA as best they could and tried to soundcheck it, all in a matter of minutes. They got it up and running and we got a microphone working again. But the boys needed to get rid of all the club's microphones and put ours up as best that they could behind the curtain before Paul Daniel's said, "Ladies and Gentlemen, I introduce to you our next act, Clubsound." When the curtains finally opened, we were in bits. The PA was squealing, but we tried our best to play through it. But as we played, half of us remembered some of the cuts we'd done in rehearsals and half of us didn't. We had seventeen minutes of what turned out to be absolute hell. We battled through it. The audience were wonderful as they still applauded. But we knew, that deep down, we had blown it. Eventually the mystery was resolved at the end of the night when one of the road crew came up and said, "What actually went wrong with the PA system?" And our roadie looked round before he said, "Here's what's wrong — a fuse has blown" Our faces dropped because we knew that this could have been replaced in a matter of minutes. So, our chance of going to Las Vegas had disappeared. But it turned out that Charles Mathers hadn't turned up anyway.

The famous magazine for showbiz was called *The Stage*. This variety paper was sold all over Britain. In the middle pages of their next issue after the Charles Mathers no-show, they said that this had been the biggest night of the year at Jolly's nightclub. Their heading read:

"They Might be Irish, But They Saved the Show."

And there were photos of all the roadies carrying the PA in front of all the dignitaries. I cannot help thinking, that if we had been able to go on that show and perform perfectly, then chances are that we would have been massive in England. Despite what had happened, we put it all behind us and we carried on. The show must go on, as they say.

We were still a success in England, but Jack would still share his dreams of going to Vegas and never returning home. Even though Jack's ideas seemed out of reach, they gave us inspiration, as we always had the safety of our families at the back of our minds. Belfast and surrounding towns were still not that safe, even for families during the Troubles. One never got far without an army road block. Cars were inspected and sometimes taken apart in the search for weapons or bombs. After dark, very few people left their homes, as they never knew if they would get home again.

The famous Belfast Opera House, designed by the most prolific theatre architect of that period, Frank Matcham, opened way back in 1895 and was called the Palace of Varieties for several years. Sadly, Belfast's cream of architecture was blown up one night as well as the Europa Hotel. The Opera House didn't get hit by a bomb, but it was caught up in the blast and badly damaged because it was right beside the hotel. The Europa Hotel became renowned for being one of the most blown-up hotels in the world. The damage to the Opera House was so severe that the owners decided to close it down for a time.

We realised that the children of the Troubles had never attended a pantomime and the majority had never even heard of one. Tommy Thomas, during his time with us, had written a small pantomime that had been performed at the Railway Bar in Antrim. Based around the story of *Cinderella,* it was called, *Cinderella — The Boot Who Lost Her Shoe.* It was based on working-class girls who worked in Gallagher's cigarette factory. I played the part of Cinderella and the two ugly sisters were two girls who worked in Gallagher's.

We contacted the Scott brothers, who were from a Jewish family and had done much for show business in Northern Ireland. They owned two theatres, the New Vic in Belfast and the Tonic Theatre in Bangor. Because of the Troubles and the opera house being closed down, we realised that the children were missing out on an annual pantomime that we'd all grown up with and loved. So, we came up with an idea and suggested to the Scott brothers that we could run a mini pantomime as part of a Christmas extravaganza show with lots of Christmas songs. They leapt at the idea. The Tonic Theatre was the biggest single standing theatre of its time and held about two thousand people. We named the show:

CLUBSOUND CHRISTMAS EXTRAVAGANZA

FEATURING CINDERELLA PANTO

After months of working with the Scott brothers, Alf and Sid, we worked hard to make everything different on stage, just to give it a Christmas feel. We even made our own props and scenery, and the Scott brothers joined in until late at night and helped us make the scenery. The week came around and we wondered if we would even get a hundred people. But to our amazement, two thousand people gathered every night for six nights. We were sold out every night.

Ironically Frank Carson returned to Belfast the following year when the Opera House reopened. "I'm bringing panto back to Belfast," he said and we smiled.

CHAPTER 8

America Here We Come

Our manager, Jack Rogers, sat us down one day and said, "I have some good news and some bad news for you. Which would you prefer first?" As usual, we responded, "The bad news." "I have some news for you regarding Las Vegas — you're not going," he said. "Is there any good news?" we chirped. "Well," he said, "Miami and Florida are opening up and the dollar is now three times higher than the pound. The Americans don't want to visit there in the summer because it's too hot for them, but the English are going, and I think you guys should go too. Because the English are going, the hotels need to provide entertainment at night." All the hotels along the strip, wanted to cater for all the English who were coming at that time of year. The hotels were putting on acts such as, Hope and Keen, a British comedy double act, Mike and Bernie Winters and The Barron Knights; all English acts who were popular at the time and that the English would be familiar with. This is what gave Jack the idea, so he contacted a man called Sidney Rose. He was an agent that had previously looked after The Bee Gees and The Who. Sidney thought that it was a great idea to take an Irish show to Miami because there were a lot of Irish people who holidayed in America as well as English people. We needed to put on a great stage show, so Jack drafted in a guy called Norman Maine from the Portrush area in Northern Ireland. He was a quiet man, although no one in Northern Ireland had really heard of him. He had choreographed and directed amazing acts from around the world. He had also directed different acts for Top of the Pops and Barbara Streisand, and a show called Hallelujah Hollywood. For four or five years, he had directed and produced for The Royal Variety Show; and yet Jack managed to persuade him to direct and choreograph us. We hit the news again in Northern Ireland. *Clubsound are going to America.* Our very own famous Northern Ireland TV presenter, Gloria Hunniford, interviewed us on her show. After all the planning, we arrived in May 1981, to rehearse with Norman Maine and launched the show in June. The venue where we performed our shows was the Marco Polo Hotel. It had a large conference centre that held about nine hundred people. We named the show, *The Blarney Boys' Show*. Always at the back of our minds, we were thinking that this could be our ticket away from Northern Ireland and the Troubles. A number of people thought we were mad because of the temperatures, but these hotels were crying out for people to go there. A lot of other bands were given the chance to go as well and Jack wasn't going to miss out on taking us. When we arrived, we were treated like royalty, and asked to go on various television programmes to advertise the show.

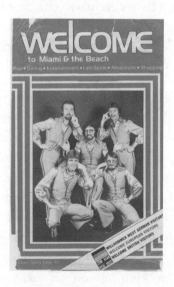

Miami promotion poster.

Ted Rogers, who was the star of Three, Two, One, was our British guest star and PP Arnold, who was a massive pop star at that time, was our American guest star. So, we started work with this top choreographer and producer, who believed in only the best. We rehearsed solidly for three weeks, starting at ten every morning. Norman laughed because some of us were definitely not dancers. Because we were from Northern Ireland, like him, he loved us dearly and persevered with us. He had an affectionate name for us and called us his *clod hoppers* because of how bad we were; but he managed to transform us into dancers. It was a different kind of Clubsound now; ultra-professional in brand new suits and ready for action. We even had original songs written for us to sing on the show and these were written by a top songwriter called Ronnie Cass, who wrote for Tom Jones. They were about the Irish living in America. Everything was set, we were ready to open the show. It was a fabulous cabaret room, but suddenly, about a week before we were about to perform, the pound crashed against the dollar. It dropped from about $2.50 to $1.30. Spain and other countries in Europe were offering a better exchange rate, so the majority of British people who used to go to Miami, chose to go to Europe instead. This had a detrimental effect on the hotels on the strip in Miami. In fact, some of them were so empty, that they drained their swimming pools.

Like the majority of British acts, we were stuck there because we had contracts. Instead of the hotels being full, they were becoming emptier. We were about to launch a press evening that was scheduled the night before our opening performance and a preview of our show had been set up in the cabaret room in the hotel where we sang at night. When the curtains opened for the preview show, we were totally taken aback; over five hundred people from the media, had piled into the room. We were very nervous. "Just go out and do your thing, they will love you," Norman Maine said. We had confidence in what he said and what he had done for us, so we went out and let them decide for themselves about our music and songs. When we had finished, each person from the media, gave us two standing ovations; we were overwhelmed. As we came off the stage, Norman whispered as he gave us a bottle of champagne. "My Clod Hopper darlings, you'll never go home again; you have made it." And we believed him.

The next day our names were all over the newspapers and on the television, and we had wonderful reviews. We had become famous in Miami and we eagerly awaited a packed house for our opening night.

When the night came, Ted Rogers went on stage to open the show and then PP Arnold sang. We were in the dressing rooms and were totally unaware of what was going on. When it came to our part on the show, the curtains opened and we walked on to the stage. We waited for huge applause and a roaring crowd, but it was awfully quiet. The lights came on as we struck the first note and gazed around to see about ninety people spread across the nine hundred seat cabaret room. Our mouths dropped as we wondered what had happened. We continued our show and did our utmost to do everything that Norman Maine had taught us. The ninety people who were there stood up and loved it, but we came away feeling totally deflated.

Like the rest of the hotels in the area, we persevered, in the hope that it would pick up. Unfortunately, the British holidaymakers were going home, because the pound continued to drop. A lot of the major acts in the hotel went home, but Jack Rogers was thoroughly convinced that we would make it. So, we continued from June through to September, and even took cuts in our wages. But it got to a point towards the end of September, that Jack couldn't finance it anymore. In actual fact, he had mortgaged his hotel, unbeknown to us, to try to keep us there; this was something that we didn't find out about for a long time. But the irony was, that because we were getting such wonderful reviews in the papers, the Americans were coming up to us and saying, "If you guys can hang on till the beginning of October, then the Americans will start their vacations. This place will be packed and you guys will go down a storm." But sadly, we didn't have enough money to stay until then and we had to go home. We were very grateful to the people who helped us — Jack Rogers, Norman Maine, Sidney Rose and Doctor Martin McAleese. Martin was involved with Air Florida, alongside his wife, Mary, who later went on to become the president of Ireland. We knew that they had been on holiday in the area, so we contacted Martin, who was unable to help us financially, but he was able to arrange for Air Florida to sponsor our flights home. Upon our arrival home in Northern Ireland, the local media took the opposite stance to the US media. The newspapers lambasted Clubsound as failures. It was hard to believe; we had left on so much of a high when we went to America. Yet, here we were, coming home with our tails between our legs. The only exception, in the midst of that onslaught, was Eddie McElwaine of *The Belfast Telegraph*. He shared our story on a two -page spread, and featured an interview with me. Gloria Hunniford also showed her support by inviting us on her television programme again. This gave us the opportunity to explain to the public what had happened.

Miami newspaper extract

We felt as if we were back where we started, and wondered if we would ever make it to the top. We struggled on our return and the band never seemed to take off again. I didn't know what to do at that time. Then Jack Rogers asked me if I would go solo? I did go solo for one year and Clubsound and I parted company. Billy Bingham, the guitar player, went back to South Africa. He had met a girl there and decided to marry her. Between 1983–84, I tried a year on my own, but I didn't like it; it just wasn't the same. One night, we were booked to play in the same club; Clubsound and myself. I was doing a solo comedy act and Clubsound were performing as well. When I finished, I was asked by one of the guys if I would come back. I returned gladly; I had missed the band and the camaraderie.

Clubsound on the Krankies LWTV.

Once I re-joined, it was as if I'd never been away and we started to rehearse regularly. The band became popular once again. In the midst of one of the rehearsals, it was as if God was guiding us again with a break. A call came from London Weekend Television; it was their producer Noel Green. He had directed us once when we did a television programme for RTE, Ireland's National Television. "Is your band

still going?" he asked. "Of course it is," I replied. "I'm going to give
you a live spot on *The Kranky Show* on prime time Saturday night,"
he replied. We featured alongside other acts such as Suzi Quatro and
Modern Romance, but we were the only act that actually performed
live. Noel thought we were wonderful, so he gave us a top spot with
The Krankies. From that point on, the band took off again.

CHAPTER 9

Radio Meets Belfast Sadie

My radio broadcasting career started way back in the seventies when a guy called Brian McSherry and all the guys from Downtown Radio, heard the band in The Railway. A new radio station had been launched in March, 1976, called Downtown Radio and, Brian, who was one of the presenters from the Republic of Ireland, hosted the afternoon programme. With Northern Ireland being such a small place, lots of radio presenters, including Downtown Radio, came to hear Clubsound from different places. Brian thought that we were really funny and he asked Tommy and if we would come into the studio and do these little comedy characters because the band was well known and the people loved it.

It became our opening to radio and the comedy proved to be very popular as we had a lot of laughs doing these programmes with Brian. "Have you ever thought about doing radio yourself?" Brian asked one day. I said that I'd never thought of it. "There's a Sunday show that all the radio presenters are obliged to do now and again," Brian replied. Secretly, no one wanted to do it because they were already working five days a week. "We actually have to split it with daytime presenters, but I think that you could do it if I showed you," he added. This sounded like an amazing opportunity. I decided to give it a go and he trained me on how to work the desk and the radio station. It was a success and I ended up broadcasting that show every Sunday night, for the next three years, from 1977 to 1980. This show ended up being a forerunner to my radio broadcasting career.

In 1985, four or five of us had a holiday break in a chalet at Killyhevlin Hotel in Enniskillen. We were sitting outside on the jetty, having a drink and talking about our plans; how long we thought we would stay as a band and what our future plans were, when all of a sudden, a cruiser pulled up beside us. "Would you mind if I use your restroom as ours is broken?" a female voice asked. Of course, being gentlemen, we said yes. "I know your face, are you not the one in Clubsound?" The woman asked when she came out. I replied that I was. "Did you used to be on Downtown radio, back in the seventies?" she asked. I explained that I gave it up when I went to Miami. She spoke about how she used to listen to me on Sunday nights and suggested that I should go back on the radio. "Would you like to come and meet my husband on the cruiser?" she asked. "Yes, that would be very kind," I replied. Her husband, Martin Dillon was a famous author; he'd written lots of books on the Troubles and was the Editor of BBC Radio Ulster at the time. Happily, we all went out and after a few drinks, she shared with him how brilliant I had been to listen to me on the radio and said that he should give me a job. Martin asked if I was looking for a radio job. "I'm always open for anything," I replied with a laugh. The conversation ended and I thought no more about it. It was like God guiding things again; it was unreal. It was similar to God guiding us in London when we had a chance meeting with Don Charles and The Monarchs back in the sixties; and God working through my sister when I was a child; and again, when I left South Africa and was drawn to come home because of my father's death. I know now that it was God telling me that I needed to come home, even though my dad didn't want me to. It was as if I was being guided even though I didn't realise it at the time.

After my experience with Downtown Radio, I anticipated that joining the BBC would be similar, but not so. A few weeks later, Bob Crooks, the senior producer for the BBC, phoned me. "I've been speaking with Martin Dillon and he thought you would be interested in doing some radio?" he said. I was totally gobsmacked as I didn't expect anything to come from my chance meeting with Martin. "I haven't done anything on radio in about four years," I replied. He seemed unperturbed. On Radio Ulster there was more talk and discussion with very little pop music played. Paul Clark was doing the afternoon show and playing what little amount of pop music there was. "Paul Clark is taking some time off for a holiday for two months. Could you fill in for him?" he asked. After ensuring that I would be paid, I agreed. So, they brought me into the studio, gave me two producers and a researcher, and that was the beginning of my broadcasting career with the BBC.

While Paul Clark had been putting his stamp on his own show, I was the one now hosting it. There wasn't a chance of me mirroring his style as I am my own person with my own individual approach. I knew that I couldn't be Paul Clark, I could only be me, so I decided that I would just be myself. I hadn't done radio for years. I'd only been on Downtown and everything I did on that programme was my own creation; now I had to do what the producers wanted so I felt as though I was in a straitjacket. I finished the two months and they told me that Paul Clark was leaving to go onto television and asked if I would I interested in a job I agreed and named the show, *The Afternoon Show with George Jones.*

On the first day I arrived, there was a big discussion between the two producers about what shape the show should take. My two producers were Pauline Crooks and Cherrie McIlwaine, who had one of the best broadcasting voices ever to come out of Northern Ireland. However, after the discussion it was decided that I should just roll with the show and see what happened. Even though the BBC had a better set-up for interviews and news, I gently began playing more music. However, everything seemed to be controlled from above with no margin for individual style.

Then, a new presenter called John Bennett, was introduced to Radio Ulster. He took the place of Walter Love, in the afternoons where I was scheduled. This led to me being moved to the weekend, with Friday afternoons, Saturday mornings and then Sunday morning shows. I invented my own special Sunday morning show, which was called, *GJ — a.m.* It was designed to draw in a younger audience by playing music that was in the charts. I was being produced then by my good friend, Bob Crooks, who was on the same wavelength as me about playing more chart music.

The show ran from 1985 through to 1988/89, but I wasn't totally happy. With two producers, I just felt restrained and over-produced because I couldn't be myself. I wanted to do what the public wanted, as I'd done on the stage with all the characters, comedy, and light heartedness. I had to constantly take instructions from the producers which left no room for creativity. I had been receiving positive feedback from my radio programme on the streets, but the main question asked was, "Why are you not telling us your jokes on the radio? Why can't you be you? Let us hear those comedy characters." And similar comments.

Over a period of time, of sharing good humour with listeners, I was persuaded to introduce more comedy by telling jokes. It was then that I invented Belfast Sadie. She was a woman I invented and she really took off. She was a character who was just a figment of my imagination, but she was real to the listeners. It was as if I had become a ventriloquist. People used to ask if they could speak to Sadie and I invented things such as Sadie's Weather which I pre-recorded, and I'd leave gaps so that I could talk to her live and fill in with her recording. She read out poems that people sent in as well in her special accent and it was really funny. We called it *Cultural Corner.*

But no matter how successful Sadie was at drawing listeners; the powers that be said Sadie had to retire. That threw me completely and made me more disillusioned with my weekend shows. I secretly longed to be the character who they wanted and by the time it came to 1990, I was in the frame of mind to leave Radio Ulster.

Belfast Sadie, giving George a piece of her mind.

At the start of the new decade, there was another change in the leadership at Radio Ulster, with Robin Harris taking on a management role as head of programmes. With a fear of being dropped, I thought to myself that this would be a good time to leave radio and go back into Clubsound. However, Robin called me into his office and spoke to me about my slots on the radio and how they were doing. After reviewing the figures and different aspects of the show, Robin asked if I had any plans. "I've actually been seriously thinking about packing it in," was my initial response. "No, no, no, you can't do that. What is it that you really want to do on radio?" he replied. "I want to be on five days a week instead of the weekends. I want to do a daytime broadcasting show and I want to be left alone. I just want someone to work with me instead of me working for them. But the main thing I want, is just to be me and basically do what I do on stage but through radio," I replied. He paused. "What sort of time are you talking about?" he asked. "I'd like to do the four to five afternoon slot — the drive home slot." I replied. "That's a very difficult time because Radio Ulster is news orientated. Would you even be able to get people to listen to you?"

he asked. "I'm sure that this would work, and I can help people drive home safely; a parent making the dinner, a little crack on a stressful day goes a long way," I said with confidence. "I'll make you a deal. I'll bring you on for five days a week, during the hour you've requested, but on one condition," he said. Oh no, I thought, here we go, the mat is going to be pulled from under me. Astonishingly, his condition was that I had to bring back Belfast Sadie. It was then that I realised that this guy knew what the people of Northern Ireland wanted to listen to on radio and … I had to convince Sadie to come out of retirement.

The one-hour show became so successful that I was asked if I would do three-thirty to five. A short time later, I was called back again. They wanted me to extend my programme from three to five in the afternoon.

Shortly after that time, I received the news that my radio programme had been short-listed along with three other finalists, for the UK Sony Award. The previous award winner had come from Radio Ulster as well, and this was Connor Bradford and his producer. They gave such a long acceptance speech, naming practically everyone in the world, that the audience was exhausted. When it came to my announcement, the announcer said, "I do hope that it's not going to be another long speech, because it's another Radio Ulster winner. It's George Jones who wins the best local radio presenter of the United Kingdom."

I went on stage and walked up to the microphone. "As I came up here, I heard comments such as, Oh no, not Radio Ulster again, should we just book a room for the night? But no, I won't take long. It's such an honour for me to accept this award, especially at a time when our wee country is going through so much trouble and violence. I see this as an award not just for myself but for my listeners and the team, because what we were trying to do in the programme was escape the darkness by having just a few minutes of laughter." This was one of the proudest moments of my life when I won this award, not only for myself but for Northern Ireland too. This was yet another gift that God had blessed me with.

When I returned home around ten that night, our house was empty and in darkness, but something weird was happening. We were still in the midst of the Troubles, anything could be going down, and then … suddenly out of nowhere all the lights came on and people jumped out from everywhere. "Surprise! Surprise!" they shouted. It was such a shock that I didn't know if I had wet myself or not.

The next few days, letters and cards of congratulations arrived from all over the world, including the local paramilitaries. What shocked me was they didn't even use a code word![6]

It was then that I introduced surprise calls to people. Let me give you a few examples …

I would phone people and pretend to be the gas man. We had letters that came in from people asking me to do this. They wanted to play a trick on their friends. Then I would have to inform them that we were live on-air. I had to use different voices so people wouldn't recognise me. I would do various voices, for example: American, Asian, English and Scottish accents. There were many people who wrote in and said that they had a friend who was a real prankster. They wrote, We want you to get him because he's always getting us and he will never be pranked by anybody and get away with it."

The guy who they wanted me to call rented out property in the Queen's University area, so I rang him and pretended that I wanted to rent a house and said that I was coming to live in Northern Ireland, with a big family and two dogs. He kept saying things such as, "I don't think that will work." "Do you not want me to rent your property?" I replied. "No, no, of course not," he replied. So, I kept him going for a long time. "This is a very special day for me because I want to reveal that I'm George Jones, and you're live on-air, on Ulster Radio and everyone's listening," I said in an unusual accent. "What?" he shouted

6 Northern Ireland paramilitaries issued a code word and that code would confirm if the instruction was correct. Example: If a bomb was placed in a location, they would phone a newspaper and using the code word, and they would inform the newspaper of the location. This allowed the security forces to know if it was genuine or a hoax call.

and slammed down the phone. The boys rang me straightaway. They were thrilled.

I did lots of those kinds of calls, where I had to pretend to be somebody else at the request of a listener who had written in to the show. Although sometimes they backfired. There is a great story about this woman and her husband. I think it was coming up to their golden wedding anniversary. They were so much in love, and this wee man had written a lovely letter.

"Would you please surprise my wife on our anniversary?" he wrote.

It was on a Saturday and he had booked the entire weekend at Kendal in the Lake District, and a tour for the whole weekend. This is how it can sometimes go wrong and you have to be really ready. The letter arrived on a Tuesday with instructions to read it out on the Friday. The anniversary was on the Saturday but they'd be away in Kendal. My producer was Liz Kennedy. "Now treat this nice and gently," she said, to which I agreed. I knew that this man loved his wee wife as he'd written this lovely letter and it was very special. So, I rang up and pretended I was from the tour company. "Hello love, I believe that you're going to be spending the weekend with us in the Lake District. Well, when we stop on one of the days, we're going to have a picnic and karaoke, and we're going to sing lots of songs. What we want to know is, would you like to sing your favourite song?" I said in an English accent. "And we'll have your karaoke track ready. We're asking all our guests to do that; would that be alright?" There was a long pause. "To tell you the truth, son, we'll not be going that weekend," she replied. "I'm sorry to hear that. Why aren't you going?" I replied. "Well, my husband died on Wednesday," she replied. I saw Liz Kennedy turn white behind the screen. I'd received the letter on Monday of that week. So, we were totally unaware of what had happened during the week. I held myself together and decided to keep up the English accent. "Well, I'm terribly sorry to hear that and I understand why you can't go and our deepest apologies from the tour company. We wish you all our sympathies and goodbye," I said. As soon as I ended the call, I had to explain to the audience that sometimes this is what happens when it's live. We were obviously unaware that this dear lady's husband had passed away. Meanwhile, Liz rang the lady's sister who had helped the gentleman write the letter and they understood perfectly. People rang in to offer their condolences and they were very kind. That was a true example of the necessity of being ready for anything on live radio. Ironically, a year later, I was doing a concert in Belfast, and while people were taking their seats before the concert, a lady ran up and hugged me. "This is lovely, but why are you hugging me?" I asked. "I'm the lady you rang up and surprised on my anniversary, the week my husband died. And when you thought it might have been wrong to do so, that phone call brought me so much love and joy, that before he died, my husband had taken the time to arrange this wonderful thing," she said. This was a lovely surprise that I got to meet her. Just when I thought that I'd done something wrong, it actually turned out to be something beautiful.

Another time, I had a guy ring from Scotland. "How are you doing, Jock?" I said. "Well, I'm not doing very well today," he replied. "What's wrong?" I asked him. "Well I'm lonely. I'm going through this bad depression, and I'm really thinking of ending it either today or tomorrow," he replied. "Well hold on Jock, you know you can't give up," I said, desperate to help him. At this stage, I was really stuck, but I couldn't give up on him. "Well, what's the problem, Jock?" I asked. "Well, I don't have any friends," he replied. "Well, stop right there, because while I'm talking to you, the phones are lighting up and there's people here who want to be your friend. There are people who want to write to you and meet up with you. Now, don't do anything stupid, we're all behind you. You're in Scotland and we're in Northern Ireland. So, I'm going to ring you on Friday and I'm going to ring you on Monday, and I'm going to ring you every day if necessary," I said. After speaking to him he seemed alright. "Now Jock, you're not going to do anything stupid, are you?" I said. "No, I'm not," he replied. Almost immediately, we had people lined up wanting to contact him. A year later, Jock wrote to me saying that I had saved his life and he'd become a Christian. This news warmed my heart and gave me faith in radio.

Not all radio broadcasts, as I found out, were happy occasions. I was really put to the test, as were my fellow presenters, on that fateful day on 15th August, 1998, when the IRA placed a car bomb at Omagh and tragically, many lives were lost. Just when everyone was trying to work together for peace, there seemed to be a step back into the horror of what had come before. On the Saturday when it happened, I was filming Town Challenge, in a town called, Ardglass. It was in the afternoon and we had a huge crowd. Suddenly, the news filtered through about what had happened in Omagh and the crowd slowly drifted away. We had completed the filming, and as I drove home, I remembered that I had a radio programme coming up on the Monday. People normally expect me to be jolly, have lots of laughs and include surprise calls. All I could think was, how am I going to approach this? I phoned Ian Kennedy to ask for his advice. "George, it's a tragedy, but the best thing that you can do is just be yourself; you can handle it," he said. At the time, I thought to myself that yes, it's going to be different this week, but I can handle this. I believe that this was one of the most significant times that God was with me, during the disaster of the Omagh bomb. It was a miracle how I managed to keep going in the midst of so much trauma. I can see now, how God was guiding and strengthening me to broadcast to the people. I decided to open the microphones, and I remember to this day that I began the show with, "Well, good afternoon, everyone. Normally at this stage, we'd have a couple of hours of fun coming up, but as the country knows, we've been hit with this devastating news and tragedy of innocent people losing their lives. I don't really know how to do this programme, except play you some music and allow you to give me your comments, through me on radio. I don't actually know what music to play, but I'm going to open up with this …" I played a song from Nancy Griffiths, called, *From a Distance*. Nancy sings, *From a Distance, the world would be a better place* and she repeats the line, *God is watching you*. I nearly broke into tears while I was addressing the people, but I believe now that God helped me to continue and ideas for songs began to pour into my mind. After playing a few songs, the phone lines became busy with people ringing in to offer their condolences. Not only were there tears on the other end of the phone; tears also fell in our studio. At the close of the programme, I played the hymn, *Amazing Grace*. This continued every night for a week, and at the end of each evening, I was like a sponge; you could have wrung me out; I felt like a conduit, expressing people's sympathies live on-air. It was the same for all my colleagues and others presenting shows; it was a very emotional time. At the end of one of the programmes, I remember Pat Loughery, who was the controller at the time, putting his hands on my shoulders as a gesture of support. I was in tears by the end of every day.

It was a really touching moment when I received a beautiful letter from the Archbishop Robin Eames, for helping the people get through that time. He had been writing letters of condolence to the people every day and said what a wonderful thing it was that we were doing. It was at that time that Radio Ulster was put forward for the UK Sony Award for the way that they handled the disaster. I received calls from lorry drivers, who had stopped and were crying. One had some poetry and I asked him to read it out. I got a letter from one of the surgeons in the hospital, telling us who the real heroes were; the ones bringing in the badly injured, when they were bleeding themselves. It was just an incredible expression of sympathy from Northern Ireland and the world to Omagh. I decided at this point that I needed to visit Omagh to pay my respects. On the Wednesday, I received flowers, and Hilary and Natalie decided to come down with me. When we got there, we saw flowers everywhere. Prince Charles had visited and brought flowers too. Obviously, with being on the radio and in Clubsound over the years, I was well known there. I drove into a hotel car park that I knew and we decided to walk around Omagh. Bearing in mind, that I had looked at the photographs of all the people in the newspaper, who had lost their lives. I was feeling really thankful that I hadn't known anybody personally, but I still felt sympathy for the families. When I walked across the car park with my family, this lady ran up to me. "George, hello, how are you? I listen to you every day and it's so wonderful that you've come down to Omagh. Isn't it awful?" she said. "Yes, it is, it's a tragedy. We're here to show our respects," I said. "Well, that's very good of you. Isn't it a shame about that poor lady? You knew her, didn't you?" she said. "No," I replied. And then my mind started racing, as I couldn't think who she meant. "She's the girl who you rang up the day before her wedding day. She was one of your surprise calls," she said. Then suddenly, it hit me, that I had known this girl and now she was dead. Her fiancé had written in and wanted to surprise her. She had been so excited to be mentioned on the radio and the next thing I knew, she was a victim.

That is what live radio does for you. At the end of that week, I said to myself I didn't ever want to go through a week's broadcasting like that again. It was a very tearful time and every radio presenter in the area felt the same. Some of the stories that were related to me that week were just horrendous. Radio Ulster, as you may be aware, reached out across the world. But the output of sympathy from around the world and from Northern Ireland that came flooding in for Omagh, was incredible.

Omagh Bomb, August 15, 1998. Killed 29 people and injured 220 people.

CHAPTER 10

An Opening to Television

After the radio programme was extended to a two-hour show in the afternoon, it grew in popularity. Sadie had become a great star, and I was introducing new characters and new features to the show. As well as the surprise calls, I had introduced a new feature, which was to ask people to call in and tell us the furthest place that they were calling from; which was like gathering people in to show us the range and distance that the radio was reaching. We then sent our listeners a little prize as a reward. At the time, we also had Radio Ulster car stickers, which were really popular. People put the stickers on the rear window of their cars to show which radio station that they were supporting. I asked listeners to request their free car sticker, and asked them to take it wherever they travelled and put it in the most obscure place that they could find, take a photograph of it and send it back to us. This received a huge response that we weren't expecting. We even received photos of stickers stuck to trees in the outback of Australia. We had them stuck to the Great Wall of China and one with Niagara Falls in the background. Anywhere people could take one and put it up on their travels, was welcomed. Or, they could send in a photo to show how far away they lived from Northern Ireland. The most incredible photo was of a guy who worked in the Norwegian Fjords. He stuck a sticker to the glass dome of a submersible, about forty or fifty fathoms under water. Here was Radio Ulster in a little submersible. Another one was an American coastguard in Alaska, who patrolled up and down the edge of Canada and Russia. The Americans and the Russians actually spoke to each other, along the border. The coastguard very proudly showed me a photo of him wearing his sticker on his uniform. I told him that I thought that was wonderful and that I loved the work the coastguard was doing. He sent me some beautiful American coastguard sew-on badges that you put on uniforms. I asked him if there was any animosity between the Americans and the Russians. He said that there wasn't and that they were just patrolling the waters. I told him that I'd always loved Russian hats and that it would be great to go skiing in one. As a lovely gesture, he sent me a Russian fur hat with a red star on it. These were the kinds of wonderful stories that were happening through the power of radio.

I continued with the surprise calls that were becoming more and more outlandish. As a consequence, I was running out of characters to pretend to be. Everyone had heard so much about the calls that their popularity grew. There was now such a vast number of listeners, that everyone became wary of me phoning them on their birthday. I have actually met people on the street years later, who said, "You caught me back in those days and I've never forgiven you." I still get that today.

I used to do really off the wall things on the radio. If someone was ringing me from their car, I was aware that you weren't allowed to use your phone while driving, so I always asked them to pull in to the side of the road. I would ask them if they wanted to enter a competition, but first of all I asked which road they were on. Then I would ask them for the make, model and colour of their car. Once they told me I asked them to turn on their hazard lights, so I could try an experiment. For example, I would say, "If anyone is driving around on Holywood Road and they see a red Volkswagen Golf, with its hazard lights on, toot your horn." As I was talking to the person, all I would hear was car horns from drivers passing by. It was amazing.

The programme continued to grow in popularity and the show went from 1991 through to 1995. I was then asked to go to the head of programmes' office. The head controller at the time was Pat Loughery. All I could think was, oh no, what have I done wrong. I was worried because at that time I was working for the BBC on contract. "Pat, what have I done wrong?" I asked. "Oh nothing, nothing wrong. I'm delighted with the show, it's doing wonderfully well. The problem is there's have been slight changes to the BBC Charter, and we've been obliged to offer work to the independent sector for input supply to the BBC. I was thinking that your programme is so self-contained because there is only you and a producer that you could possibly go independent." I wondered what that meant. Was I going to have to set up a company? I didn't want to be involved in looking after accounts, VAT, and everything that goes with it. "Will you please go away and think about it as this would really help us out. We have to offer a certain percentage of our programmes to the independent sector," he said. Before the changes to the BBC Charter, it was only in-house who were able to do programmes. But the Charter had to be changed to allow this to be open to independent companies. A lot of the programmes needed to become independent and mine was one of them.

I remembered that there were two guys I knew, Ian Kennedy, who had been a producer and ex-head of programmes on BBC in Northern Ireland and John Nicholson, who was originally head of agriculture, and later became the head of television. They had set up an independent company called Straight Forward Productions. So, I thought that I should get Ian's advice as I had worked with Ian at the BBC before he left. He had been head of programmes at one stage. So, I rang Ian. "Tell me this, would you be interested in taking my programme on as I am currently on contract to the BBC and I don't want to set up my own company," I said. He agreed and asked me to come down and see him and John. That was in 1995, and the programme became known as, *Just Jones*. We were allocated the same time between 3–5 p.m. and the company supplied its own producer. We were no longer on the actual radio floor, but we were given our own office. Liz continued as my producer and Janet Dougan was our researcher and secretary.

So, that was our team, the three of us. It became Straight Forward Productions *presents Just Jones in the afternoon*. The programme really started to kick off.

Soon after, I started to become involved in different ventures with Ian Kennedy, who asked me to do some television. He produced a series called Star Treks, which was about the lives of local personalities. It was like a biopic documentary. The series was being produced for UTV, which was actually the opposition, but Ian Kennedy produced television programmes through several different outlets. I participated in one of these programmes which took me back to Heidelberg, where I'd been with The Monarchs. It was a great opportunity to meet up with people who I hadn't seen since I'd been there when I was a young man. I was filmed walking through the streets and reflecting on the occasions and places that I had visited back in the sixties. Heidelberg Hauptstraße (main street), no longer had trams running down it, but had been changed to a pedestrian area. The director's plan was to film me walking from the end of the street towards the camera. I was quite small, like a speck, on the lens, and I had to walk the whole way up the street. Once I got to the camera, I was asked to deliver one line which was, "Really, this place hasn't changed much." We tried this shot three times, but every time that I got close to the camera, someone would walk in front of me. Consequently, the director kept shouting, "Cut! Cut!" On the fourth attempt as I headed towards the camera, the director was saying, "It's all going well, keep walking, keep walking." We almost got the shot, when a woman ran into the middle of the street. "Why aren't you on the radio today?" she said. It turned out that she was from Belfast. Talk about a small world. This demonstrated how powerful radio was in reaching people.

My show was one episode, which formed part of a series, that was aired on a Monday evening. I wondered if anyone would be really interested in it and I didn't expect many people to watch it. Anyway, after the programme was screened, Ian was called into Ulster Television (UTV) to meet the head of programmes, who said that my programme was the most watched episode of the whole series. He asked if I would be interested in television because they had an idea for a quiz show. But, I was self-employed with the BBC, and I could only work in radio. Throughout the years that I had worked for the BBC, I had never been offered any television programmes of my own; apart from raising money for *Children in Need* on radio annually, which was linked to the television show, but I will share that later. Ian then rang and told me about the offer from UTV, which I was interested in, but I suggested he check with the BBC first. Ian took my advice and rang the woman that was the new head of programmes. He asked her if they had any plans to do any television with George in the future. "No, not really, why?" she said. He told her that UTV had plans for a new programme and they were thinking of offering it to me. "Well, I would have a problem with that," she replied. "But George works for you in radio, what is the problem with him doing TV?" Ian asked. "No, I would definitely have a problem with that," she repeated. I think that is what spurned Ian on with the idea of getting me onto television. After hearing the news that there might be problems of me working for UTV, I declined the offer and subsequently Eamonn Holmes got the job for the new quiz show.

An event organised by Airbourne, Noel Edmonds charity. Helicopters gave disabled children rides.

Two or three weeks later, I was talking to a producer called Paul Evans, who said that a television offer was going to come my way. It was to present a gameshow that would be filmed on the road. It was modelled on the basis of the old, *It's a Knockout* programmes. This was a show that was originally broadcast on national television in the sixties. The show that I was going to be hosting was called *Town Challenge*. Different towns would be playing against each other with music and lots of fun. So, I decided to sign up for it, thinking that I would be the sole presenter of the show. I didn't even find out until the first day of filming, that there were going to be dual presenters. We were still feeling unsure how the show was going to develop. The first programme of the series was filmed in Magherafelt, County Derry/Londonderry, which was the hometown of the then controller, Pat Loughery. I arrived where the show was to be filmed, and this chap Hugo Duncan, walked up to me. "Hi Hugo, are you here to do the music?" I said. "No, I'm here to present this," he replied. I have to admit, that I was shocked to say the least. I opened the script to the first page in the credits I found that it was to be a dual presentation, featuring me alongside Hugo. Nevertheless, I assigned myself to the task. The series became very popular because it was localised and everybody loved it. Hundreds of people turned up for each show and it was really successful. We filmed one series every year for three years. My radio programme was also running alongside it and also enjoying success.

Towards the end of the three years of presenting the show, I became fed up. Even though I enjoyed doing television, it was not the type of programme that I really wanted to do. What I wanted was to present a variety show in music and entertainment, like a quiz show or a chat show. So, after the third year, I said to Ian Kennedy, "I don't really want to do this." But he said to me, "It's really good for your profile though. It keeps you on television." I told him that I really wanted to do television of a different sort. Ian thought about it and approached the head of programmes. "George is thinking of pulling out of *Town Challenge* because he really wants to do television of his own." She said that this could be arranged. However, I was encouraged to do a fourth year. After this final year, Ian was allowed to film documentaries with me, which was the start of a new series. These included a documentary in Australia, which was called, *George Down Under*, one in New York, which was called, *George in the Big Apple* and finally, *George and the Queen* which was filmed with me and my band on the QE2 cruise ship, travelling to New York. The latter was made into two programmes and the whole series was extremely popular; which I will tell you more about later.

I really enjoyed doing these documentaries, but I still wanted to do a night-time variety show. So, when the fifth series of *Town Challenge* was due to be filmed, I said that I really didn't want to do another series. Once again, they encouraged me to do another series by offering me a pilot show of my own, which was called, *It's George Jones*. I was very excited about it as this was just what I wanted to do. I started working on it with Ian Kennedy, as Straight Forward Productions was going to produce it for the BBC. I was promised this pilot, the set was built and we were able to secure Engelbert Humperdinck as the top star, Norman Collier, the comedian, The Renaissance Singers and The Cellar Club, who were a great duo from Dublin. Their names were Dave Malloy and Paul McDonald and we became great friends. The show was filmed with lots of great variety performers and a bit of comedy from me. I also added a bit of rock 'n' roll with a nine-piece band, and I sang with them to a live audience. The reports were great, everybody thought it was brilliant and we were all set to go. But little did I know that there was another guy who was being offered a pilot which was going to be filmed from the markets downtown in Belfast, at the same time. I was told afterwards that he had made a series before. This made me more and more disillusioned with what was going on because I was told that my show was great, they were going to keep the set and it was all guaranteed. To my dismay, I found out later that it was already promised to this other guy; so, there was little hope of the producers changing their minds. This all led up to disillusionment of my career, but I carried on. My radio show was going well, as were my mini documentaries right through to 2005.

One of my favourite things that I used to do every year, which was an absolute delight, was to run an online auction for *Children in Need* during my radio show. The people in Northern Ireland were wonderful because they offered luxury items for auction. There were huge prizes including luxury holidays, cars, tickets to watch the Monaco Grand Prix, helicopter rides and not forgetting that every year a building company donated their latest cement mixer. This was a little obscure you might think, but the different companies were really generous. The public was also really enthusiastic at joining in with the auction and generating thousands for this worthy cause. One year, we raised eighty to ninety thousand pounds. The total money raised in the Northern Ireland region was £250,000, so the auction had managed to contribute a substantial portion towards the grand total. For fifteen years, I hosted this auction for *Children in Need.*

Every year, we were asked to perform different challenges. One year, we were taken to Manchester United, which was a dream for me as I have been a supporter for over forty years. I was challenged, to score penalties against the famous Manchester United goalkeeper, Peter Schmeichel MBE. Naturally, I was excited about this, as I was a massive fan, and knowing that there would be cameras filming, I thought it would be amazing if I could score just one goal. So, prior to this event, I had contacted someone who knew how to score goals; my good friend George Best. He took me to Avoniel Leisure Centre in Belfast, to practice. On the day of the challenge, I was honoured to meet Sir Fergie, otherwise known officially as Sir Alex Ferguson CBE, the Manchester United manager; who is considered to be the greatest manager of all time. I had six chances to score past Peter and some did hit the target, but because it was all for a *Children in Need* event, I was given eleven shots in the end. After a few attempts, Fergie came over to me and whispered, "Put them all to the left as the big lad doesn't like jumping to the left." I took his advice and scored four.

From left: George Jones, Peter Schmeichel MBE and Sir Alex Ferguson CBE.

Another challenge I was given was to perform in *Riverdance*. I had to wear a Michael Flatley sparkling shirt. We made a small film of me going to London, not in front of an audience I'd like to add. We practised the end piece where all the dancers are lined up to perform the famous finale. I was sent to Irish dancing classes as this was all new to me. I thought that I just needed to learn a little bit of the dance so that I didn't show myself up. A trained champion dancer and friend, Dominic Kirwin, helped me immensely. We made the film in London and I got the shirt. We went back to Northern Ireland where I had to perform the show live on *Children in Need* with a local dance school. You have to remember, that I wasn't young at the time. This was in 2004, so I certainly wasn't young, by any means. I knew the director very well, he was my dear friend, Colin Lewis. So, before we went live, he let me rehearse this two-and-a-half-minute piece, which was full on dancing with this young girl, imitating Michael Flatley. Every time we performed it, the director said, "No George, you missed a bit. Can you do it again?" I would perform it again, and he would say, "No, we need another couple of shots." In the end, I said, "Hold on a minute, have you any idea of my age? My legs are like jelly." But I managed it somehow; we performed it live and it went very well. But later on, I found out that Colin Lewis was playing a practical joke on me by getting me to repeat the dance. I found out afterwards, that they were all laughing in the control room at my expense.

Another Children in Need challenge; George wearing a Michael Flatley shirt.

In yet another challenge, I was asked to go to Heathrow Airport and show a group of children how jumbo jets work and how an airport runs. It was amazing. But my final challenge was to dress Miss Northern Ireland for the Miss World shows. Paul Costello, who was a local fashion designer, was enlisted to help me. I'm not sure what Miss Northern Ireland thought, but I designed her dress to wear on *Children in Need* night, and later for the Miss World television show.

Around Christmas time, I organised a two-hour live radio show, from Belfast. The cast was made up of young and old people who had come on the radio show to sing and entertain me and the team, during the year. We broadcasted live from The Ulster Hall to around one and a half thousand people, on my afternoon radio show between 3–5 p.m. It was presented with the intention of giving people, young and old, an opportunity to showcase their talents. This was one of my favourite programmes and, believe it or not, it ran for ten years.

CHAPTER 11

The Highlight of My Radio Career

My radio show was going really well and I was happy with the small number of programmes that I was presenting, but I had given up on my aspirations of doing full-time television work. I decided to concentrate on my radio broadcasting, which was still doing very, very well. Gerry Anderson was on in the morning with *Talkback* which ran through to lunchtime. Hugo Duncan presented a country-style programme early in the afternoon and then it was my show later in the afternoon. The whole daytime programme, therefore, was littered with great entertainment. I was able to get all the visiting big stars on my show. I tried to make a list once and I estimate that over time, I have interviewed on BBC radio alone, nearly 260 top stars.

Liz worked hard to get all the top acts, including Johnny Mathis, Howard Keel, Andy Williams, David Gates, Don Felder, Ben E. King, Cliff Richard and Meatloaf; she was an all-round producer. Even to this day, she is still involved in journalism in our local newspapers and radio. Liz had no fear, she was able to think outside the box and when it came to producing new material, no obstacle stood in her way. She always knew how to overcome, and demonstrated that she would not be defeated when she stopped at nothing to secure prime interviews with Dionne Warwick and later, Hillary Clinton.

George with Don Felder of Eagles.

As well as interviewing, I am blessed to have worked with some amazing stars, including Shirley Bassey. I remember when we were working in a place called Blighties in Farnworth. This was a huge cabaret theatre club in Manchester. We topped the bill the whole week, but we were told that Sunday was a special night because Shirley Bassey was going to appear as the main attraction, which we were happy about. Everyone was required to go in on the Sunday to check that everything was going to work properly. So, after we did our final checks, the orchestra arrived, which believe it or not, was a twenty-five piece one. They were booked to rehearse at one in the afternoon and arrived about an hour before to set up. When the time came, there was no sign of Shirley Bassey. An hour later she arrived in a full-length fur coat, walked up to the stage, tapped the microphone and because it hadn't been set or programmed, it fed back and squealed. She grabbed the edge of her coat, swirled it over her shoulder. "Get that fixed, I'll be back in another hour," she said before she walked out and left the orchestra who had been waiting an hour for her to arrive. That was my encounter with Shirley Bassey. She was an absolute diva but an incredible performer.

When Liz Kennedy heard that the world-renowned singer, Dionne Warwick, had flown into Belfast to perform, she was determined to invite her on to my radio show. Unfortunately, Dionne's management turned Liz down, saying that she was not doing any interviews whatsoever.

I didn't think any more about it until we were broadcasting live on the radio. Liz was sitting opposite me at the other side of the window, answering calls and making sure that everything was running smoothly, when suddenly, we saw a number of people walk past with Dionne and enter another studio. At that time I was playing a song, so Liz pressed her button to communicate with me. "Did you see that Dionne Warwick has just come in?" she said. "She told us that she was not doing any interviews," I replied. So, Liz went to find out what was happening and to see if she could persuade her to come onto live radio. Unsurprisingly, Liz couldn't get anywhere near Dionne, because there was this large entourage surrounding her, which went wherever she went. But this didn't stop Liz, she slipped through them, approached the most official looking person and asked if Dionne would come on the radio. They explained that Miss Warwick had called in to use this studio as the interview was for BBC Radio 2, mainland England. The BBC was doing a documentary on Aretha Franklin and they wanted Dionne's input. "Since she's in the building, can she come up and have a few words with George as he has a big listenership. And as the concert is on tonight, it would be an added bonus for her to be on the radio here," Liz said. "No," they replied, but Liz was too close to making it happen, and she was not about to give up, so she pleaded. "Please, just go and ask her." When my studio door burst open Liz was smiling from ear to ear. "Miss Warwick will give you five minutes," she said.

Normally, for any interview I did my homework on the interviewee, but other than what I knew via the news about Miss Warwick, I had to wing it[7], as we say. I pulled out a couple of her famous tracks and put one on to get the listeners ready for the interview. Then the door opened and Miss Warwick entered and took a seat.

There was no other way to begin this dream of an interview, but to give her the best Northern Irish chat, as if she had been my friend for life. While I welcomed her to Northern Ireland, I was desperately thinking of what to say next. Then, I remembered that she had come to perform a concert in the Tonic Theatre in Bangor for the Scott brothers. When I mentioned this to Dionne, she immediately eased into the interview. We went on to talk about her family life, how she got to where she was in the world of entertainment and before we knew it, five minutes had become ten minutes and before she knew it, fifteen minutes had passed. While she was chatting, her entourage were trying to communicate to us she that she was running late. I ended the interview and put on one of her records. She reached over, took my hand and in her own unique way said, "Honey, I am glad that I came in to talk to you, this has been the most relaxing fifteen minutes that I've had in my whole tour. Thank you very much." As she got up to leave, Liz commented that she was carrying cigarettes and a lighter. Dionne turned to her and in that husky American voice, said, "Yeah, and I smoke them too, honey." And off she went.

Presenting a radio programme like this, was an amazing experience. I was given a chance to interview the stars who I had grown up admiring and my radio show gave me the opportunity to do this. I was just as excited as the people who were listening. I wish now that I had made recordings of all the people I've interviewed. I would love to have them now, just for memory's sake. The only recording that I have is one that is the closest to my heart, and that is when I interviewed The Crickets. The Crickets were the backing band for Buddy Holly, who was my idol from the fifties. The stories of how The Crickets began with Buddy

---

7 To do something without preparation.

Holly were amazing, and I had the privilege of spending one hour with them. It is one of the most memorable moments of my life.

Because Liz Kennedy was such an amazing producer, we did a number of outside broadcasts that were really, really different. We used to say to people, "If you want to invite us, we don't mind where it is; it could be a factory, a shop, a bakery — anywhere. We'll do our two-hour live show from your business." This turned out to be a great idea and we ended up doing some funny things. We did one show from an underwear factory, which was hilarious, and we did a programme from a little family-run home bakery in Lurgan. While they were making bread, we had folk groups playing and we brought music with us. We did one from my hometown of Newtownards; it was in a youth centre called The Link. And because so many people turned up to the little café inside, there were people who had to stand outside. Even the traffic was held up. So, I went out to all the cars and walked up and down interviewing all the people who were in their cars. It was wonderful. Together, we did many really obscure broadcasts outside.

As well as that, we also did broadcasts from around the world. For five years in a row, we did a live show from the Fitzpatrick Grand Central Hotel in New York, on Saint Patrick's Day. We flew out with the team and interviewed all the dignitaries who were there. The president of Ireland came on our show as he was visiting for Saint Patrick's Day. We gathered together different Irish bands who lived in New York to write the music for us. Liz had also attempted to get Hillary Clinton to come onto the show for Saint Patrick's Day. Now, the Clinton's have a strong affinity with Northern Ireland as both Hillary and Bill came over to visit during the Troubles to assist with the *peace process*. Liz thought that it would be wonderful if we could get Hillary to come on the show, as Hillary was campaigning for the New York Senate at the time. So, she wrote an email to request her presence on the show and she got an email back saying that Hillary Clinton would love to come on the show. We were excited as this was going to be broadcast live on Saint Patrick's Day. Unfortunately, it was snowing on the day and she was delayed. We received a call to say that she wouldn't be able to make it and sent an apology to all the listeners. I thought nothing of it, but this wonderful producer of mine, Liz Kennedy, was not prepared to accept that and she wrote an email to the White House, saying that she was very disappointed, but she understood, and a lot of people were really looking forward to her coming onto Radio Ulster. She also asked if there was any chance that we could get an interview with her at a later stage. We knew that it was a shot in the dark, but suddenly this email came back, saying that Hillary Clinton would love to do an interview with George, live from the White House. We were elated and immediately set about planning for the big day. It was in the newspapers the day before with the headline: *George Jones' Surprise Guest to be Hillary Clinton.* We were well prepared on the day; all the dignitaries were lined up behind the glass in the studio on the sixth floor, watching me. We were told that it was a strict eleven to twelve-minute interview only. So, I decided that I was just going to be myself, as my mother had taught me, and as I had always been on radio.

The interview began with me saying, "Hello Mrs Clinton, welcome to Belfast in Northern Ireland." "It's great to be on the radio with people who I love over there. Bill and I remember visiting," she said. We talked about family and her campaign and how it was going. And by this time, about nearly twelve or thirteen minutes had passed. Behind the glass window, I was getting the cut-throat sign. I indicated that it wasn't me who was continuing to talk, it was Hillary. So, we carried on chatting and she kept saying, "And another thing ..." I had told her about my sister researching our family name, with the Jones' back to Cromwell's time. She was interested and it was very private, it was nothing to do with politics. We talked about family life in general and how she felt about people in Northern Ireland and so on. By this time, the interview had lasted for about sixteen or seventeen minutes and Liz Kennedy was tearing her hair out. The dignitaries were also starting to look worried. I kept saying quietly to them, that it was not me, it was Hillary carrying on the conversation. In the end, I said, "Mrs Clinton, I'm going to have to wrap this up now; I know you're very busy. You've given us such wonderful valuable time. Thank you for coming on, it's been a delight talking to you." "Thank you George. And another thing, your surname is Jones. Did you know that my matriarchal name somewhere along the line, was Jones?" she said. "No! was it?" I replied. "Yes. Does that mean that we could be related?" she said. "Well, maybe somewhere along the tree of life, we could be connected somewhere," I replied. "Well, that's wonderful," she said. So, I grabbed the opportunity and I said to her, "Well look, does that mean if we're related, that the next time I'm in New York, then you'll definitely come onto the show with me?" "Definitely, and you and I will sing, *When Irish eyes are smiling, together.*" By this time, the interview had lasted for about twenty-two minutes.

Another great accomplishment, which Liz achieved, was to arrange a programme that would coincide with one of my television documentaries *George Down Under.* She tried to arrange it once again on Saint Patrick's Day. We did this in November for the following March. She tried to arrange for a television documentary and two radio programmes. I expressed my concerns to Liz, as I thought that it was a long shot. "Liz, will this work? We're a long way from home, I know there's a lot of ex-pats in Australia. You're planning to do this live outside; will we get enough of a crowd?" I said. "I'm going to fly out beforehand and look at where would be the best place to do it. You plug it like mad on the radio and tell them that if they have any relatives in Sydney, there's going to be a live George Jones show broadcast to Northern Ireland from Sydney. You'll be able to say hello to your relatives back in Northern Ireland. George will do that for you." She was full of confidence. So, I kept plugging and plugging this by saying, "Send a letter or an email back to your folks in Sydney, and tell them to turn up because at this particular venue, we're going live." The scene was set, and Liz flew over to Australia to sort out our venue. When she came back, she said that we were set up for a place beside the Sydney Opera House, right on the esplanade down by the wharf. I was pleased, but

I was still very sceptical about the whole thing. But Liz, as usual, was upbeat about it.

When the time came, we arrived with an engineering team. We had also booked some Irish and Australian bands and singers to be on the show. We arrived about eleven days before we were to go live, which enabled me to do some filming for my television documentary. While I was down there, I visited Renee, my long-lost cousin in Sydney. I hadn't seen her for years and she didn't have any idea I was coming. The film crew heard about it, followed me and filmed it. I arrived with a bunch of flowers and gave her the surprise of her life. Then we visited the Blue Mountains which were very beautiful and the Kangaroo Rescue Centre where for the first time, I was able to stroke a kangaroo. Another visit on the itinerary was to the home of the well-known wine producer, Brian McGuigan. His house was set among the beautiful vineyards in the Hunter Valley. When we arrived it was like driving up to the house that was featured on the television show, *Dallas*. We were surprised to see that on the roof of his house was corrugated iron. Apparently, this is quite typical of the roofs in Australia. Brian was extremely friendly and welcomed us to his home and we couldn't believe, that although they were multi-millionaires, his wife was in the kitchen making *doorstep* sandwiches for our lunch. Brian was a very interesting man and was convinced that his family tree went back to Clones Parish in Ireland. He felt that somewhere along the line, he might have been related to the world champion boxer, Barry McGuigan. We found that there were lots of Irish connections.

During our television filming in Sydney, we had the pleasure of visiting the head of police, who had an Irish background. We also met the mayor of Sydney, who was excited that we were there for Saint Patrick's Day. Furthermore, I had the pleasure of speaking to the guy who wrote Schindler's List, Thomas Keneally. Originally, it was called Schindler's Ark and the author had Irish and Australian connections. We interviewed him about his book, to include it on the television programme. We were taking the opportunity to film as much as we

could for the television documentary while at the same time, preparing
for the radio show.

George meeting the Belfast designer of The Governor Tower in Sydney

Two days before the show, we went down to the site to check everything
was alright. The site that Liz had arranged was at a huge Italian café
and they let us use their footpath outside, where they had a lot of tables
and chairs. Liz had also arranged to put up advertising posters that
said, *Join us on Saint Patrick's Day with George Jones live from Northern
Ireland, where you'll be* able to *say hello to your Mammy.* This was done
to attract a wider audience and it all looked wonderful, but I was still
really sceptical.

Anyway, the day arrived and we went down very early in the morning
to set up the site. We weren't expected there until the afternoon because
we were going to pre-record it and then send it back live to Northern
Ireland because of the time difference. The bands turned up, and our
sound engineers, headed by John Lunn, worked very hard with the team
and sound checked all the bands and singers. The variety acts were all
great and I was happy with the site. There were about seventy tables set

up in the sunshine, but there was still nobody there yet. Again, I said to Liz, "Are you sure we should go ahead with this? Look how many tables are laid out; are all these people going to come?" Liz, full of faith said, "Don't worry, it'll be fine. You've done enough work to drum up a great crowd." So, we decided to go for lunch, and walk around Sydney. I wasn't nervous, I just didn't want to disappoint our listeners or the show, if nobody turned up. We walked back about an hour before the show was about to begin and I couldn't believe my eyes; there were about four hundred people who had joined us. Every table was full and there was a big cheer as we walked towards the set. I opened the show with, "Ladies and Gentlemen, welcome to the programme today on Saint Patrick's Day coming live from Sydney Australia." The place erupted with a huge cheer from all these people who were connected with families from Northern Ireland. The show went extremely well, in fact, so well, that Chinese people were turning up in coach loads to visit the Sydney Opera House, but when they got off the coach, instead of going to the Opera House, they came over to see what all the music and furore was about. So, it was truly an international show on that Saint Patrick's Day. The Chinese people leapt up and down, cheering and joining in the fun. I'm not entirely sure that they knew what they were cheering for, however. It went so well, that the crowd we had attracted another crowd.

The second programme that we'd arranged, came live from the studios at ABC in Australia. It wasn't an outside broadcast, but we had brought in comedians and we'd arranged various guests. This was also a great success.

Following our triumph in Australia, we decided to take the show to Atlanta, in Georgia; to connect with the Scots-Irish people who were living there. I had also become involved with a musical at that time called *On Eagle's Wing*. I was a member of the cast which followed the flight of the Scots and Irish moving to America, during the 1600s. There were two lead singers, Peter Corry, who was a well-known Northern Ireland singer, and Scottish star, Alyth McCormack, who was an amazing singer who sang in Scottish Gaelic. I was one of the four main actors who included Marty Maguire, Paddy Jenkins and the late and wonderful actor, Mr B J Hogg. There were thirty dancers and a full, ten-piece live band. On stage during the show we were also accompanied by an award-winning full pipe band. And if that wasn't a large enough cast, when we performed at the Odyssey Arena, there was a four-hundred-piece choir on each side of the stage. The musical would have its preview in Atlanta, so Liz thought that it would be a good idea to do a radio show talking to people who were connected to the Scots and Irish. I enjoyed this musical so much, I was delighted when later in life, in 2017, I was asked to play the part of Buffalo Bill, in *Annie Get Your Gun*. This was a Northern Ireland theatre production, which was directed by Peter Corry. Yet again, I have since felt that God was listening to my desires and blessing me by providing these wonderful opportunities in my life.

Playing Buffalo Bill in Annie Get Your Gun.

CHAPTER 12

Shocked and Dumbfounded

It was 2005, the show was going well, the figures were high and there was never any problem with the contract, when, out of the blue, a new head of programmes was brought in. At that time I was still with Straightforward Productions. Ian Kennedy, as usual went in to meet the new head of programmes. We didn't know about his background, but we had heard that it wasn't in broadcasting, but in some other form of media. Ian went in to sort out my usual contract renewal, but the head of programmes just turned round and said, "I've decided not to renew George's contract." Ian was dumbfounded as the show was such a success. Unable to take it all in, Ian said, "Why are you doing this? What has George done?" "Well, George has been here now for twenty-odd years, I want to change everything in Radio Ulster and George has had his fair chance at it," he replied. When Ian rang me with the news, it was the last thing I expected to hear. I think it's fair to say, that I was utterly shocked.

At the time, I was living in a beautiful cottage with my family. We had spent all my earnings renovating it, including building the stables. In those days, it was common practice to put all your money into your property, which was an investment for the future. Clubsound was still running at the time, although we weren't as fervent as we had been, as we were now in the nineties. Clubsound had been more of a highlight in the eras of the seventies and eighties.

I really believed that my broadcasting career was set for life; the news was something that I had great difficulty accepting. I, like, Ian, was completely dumbfounded; there were just no words. Ian couldn't accept it either. "I'm going to go in tomorrow and have another talk with them," Ian said. I was in agreement, thinking that Ian was the best person to talk to the head of programmes because he was a really learned guy when it came to the BBC. Ian had come up through the broadcasting circles and knew the workings of the BBC. He used to be a producer for Gloria Hunniford on Radio Ulster and he had also been head of programmes at the BBC in South-East London. Ian went in to the office the following day to approach the head of programmes. "Do you think this is wise? You're probably going to lose a lot of listeners," he said. "I expect that, but this is something that I have to do," the head replied. Realising that he wasn't going to get anywhere, Ian walked away. The story was all over the newspapers and it was just a terrible time for me as I thought that I had failed. In the back of my mind, I knew that I hadn't, but when something like this happens, you are left wondering why. I have to say, Ian Kennedy and the whole Straight Forward team were a tower of strength for me during that time, and as I was unwilling to just leave quietly after everything we'd achieved, he managed to negotiate a six-month notice period.

I was forced to leave my radio show at the BBC when I had loved working there. It deprived me of the chance to stay on-air with my wonderful friends and listeners who I had accumulated over my twenty-one years of broadcasting.

I have decided that I am not going to share any more about the stories I heard as to why they let me go; it still remains a mystery to this day. But it won't be a surprise to learn that I had a lot of hatred in my heart and I resented the BBC for the impact that this had on me and my family at the time, especially losing our home because of the cancellation of the contract.

However, since I became a Christian later in life, I have learnt to forgive and forget. I realise that back then my dependency was on people and not on the One who opened up the doors — God.

It took me a long time to forget, many years in fact, as a lot of people would continually stop me in the street and say, "Why aren't you on Radio Ulster? We miss you." The public were under the impression that I had retired, but this was simply not true and it's what hurt me the most.

Nevertheless, I endeavoured to make the last six months the best ones. I didn't know the guy who was replacing me, but it didn't really matter. Ian was of the same mind and said, "Look, just do the best six months you've ever done." And I did. Liz Kennedy had left earlier, and her replacement was Ian's daughter, Laura Kennedy; who did an amazing job. I listened to what Ian said and did the best that I could. The figures rose yet again and with Laura's help we got some great stars on the show. During my last week, I was overwhelmed with the number of emails I received — over two thousand from all over the world. People phoned in to wish me well, expressing that it was an absolute tragedy that I wouldn't be on the BBC anymore. This included well-known stars who were saying the same thing. My producer received taped messages from various stars around the world, wishing me well, which I played on the show. It was just unbearable to think that I'd be leaving broadcasting. I had gone through the trials and tribulations of radio during the good times and the bad times. For example, the time that we were broadcasting during the Omagh bomb tragedy, which was one of the hardest weeks of my life. From all the highs and lows, it had been one incredible journey that I wasn't ready to leave.

I do believe that God has been good to me and has helped me to forgive. It was an upsetting time, not just for me but also for my family. We were faced with the difficult decision of deciding to sell our beloved home to raise capital, as we had tax bills coming in and no spare money because it had all been invested into the house. All our savings had been spent on our property as well, so we didn't even have that option. We contacted our financial advisor who offered us support and we were pleased to accept a good offer for the house, but sadly, it broke my wife's heart to part with it. It was a sad time in her life too as she loved it and had devoted so much of her time to it. Being a great interior designer, she had put so much of herself and her ideas into the house. It hurt me even more to see my family suffering after my job loss. The news continued to be reported in the newspapers for ten days, but unwittingly, they helped by supporting me as they were on my side. I was also aware that the public were behind me, as during my final week, they rang in in their droves. The phones went crazy and I felt about ten feet tall. At that stage, I began to accept that I hadn't done anything wrong. If I had been a Christian at the time, I would have been able to resolve myself in the knowledge that God had another plan for my life. But unfortunately, it wasn't yet, so it was like being in darkness and not knowing. I know now that if I had turned to him, then he would have given me the strength to continue with my life. It's always in the midst of dark and tragic times, that I believe that people need God.

I still have the large number of emails, which were sent to me at that time to offer support; I will never part with them. Eventually I moved on, when the six months sadly came to an end. Straight Forward Productions threw me a farewell party where the BBC dignitaries presented me with an ornamental crystal microphone as a leaving present. These were given out very rarely. I accepted it, feeling that I had to show respect for the company I had worked for. Everyone at the party wished me well for the future, as I finally said goodbye to the BBC in June, 2006.

It's hard to believe that the decision of just one person can have a huge impact and change the lives of many.

When I returned home, I felt beleaguered and overwhelmed. The effects of what had taken place had a huge effect on our lives. Once again, Hilary and I started from the bottom. It's amazing how the people who make these decisions don't realise the rippling effect that it has on your family. It wasn't the fact of losing my status as a celebrity because I was always one with Clubsound and I got on with my life. I never had any wish to be a massive star, but I just wanted to represent our wee country in wherever that took me, and I was willing to go.

We spoke to our daughter, who was married with two girls. Natalie lived across the road from our cottage with land next to her house, so she asked me and Hilary if we would like to build a small house there. We thought that this would be a great idea as Natalie's eyes still hadn't improved and we always had to live within close proximity to her as Hilary needed to help her out and drive her around when her husband was working. She also needed help with the horses in her stables. I had been thinking of getting one of those kit houses, like a log cabin or similar, as we needed to downsize. So, we applied for planning permission, but we couldn't get it as it was in a green belt area. What they did agree to was for us to build an apartment extension onto Natalie's house. Natalie was in favour of this, as she wanted her parents close by. We still live in the house, to this day.

CHAPTER 13

Who Said it was Over?

A few months passed before I was approached by a friend called John Rosborough, who was a well-respected man in radio circles, because he had started up many radio stations. He had worked in Downtown Radio, where I had worked back in the seventies. He had become the head of Downtown and then he had branched out to open other radio stations. He had opened a station under the auspices of UTV, called U105. It was a brand-new station situated in the buildings of Ulster Television. He asked if I would like to come on the radio. He knew what had happened to me and what I had gone through, as it had been all over the newspapers. I said to him, "I'm not ready to go back on the radio, it hurt me so much, but I don't know what I'm going to do." He thought about it, and said, "Well, why don't you keep your hand in and just do a Sunday show?" I agreed and said that I would. I asked to self-produce it and control, which I did. The show went ahead and it turned out to be very popular. It ran from September, 2006 to January, 2007. In January, John rang me and said, "The Sunday show is going wonderfully well, and the directors of UTV have just had a meeting and they've asked, that now the dust has settled, would you be prepared to go on five days a week?" I decided to think about it and I spoke to Hilary, as the money would be helpful and I needed to get back to work again. So, I came back to John. "Okay, I'll do it. What time are you going to put me on?" "The drive-time slot," he said. "But that'll be up against my old show on the BBC," I replied.

He winked. "That's the idea!" "Okay, we'll give it a try," I replied with some reluctance.

By March, 2007, the papers who had always been on my side, decided to print the RAJAR (Radio Joint Audience Research) figures. The Belfast Telegraph printed a two-page spread. On one side was a photograph of me and on the other page was a photograph of the man who had replaced me on the BBC. The article looked at the difference of the listening figures, and I had more or less doubled them. The newspaper used the headline: *Why Was This Man Paid Off?* I was flattered that the newspaper was supporting me, but I wish to convey that I wasn't gloating by any stretch of the imagination. I just felt like the circle had come round again and I was back on the radio.

I stayed at U105 for five years, but with all due respect to them, I began to feel restricted once again. Don't get me wrong, I was thankful for my job, but I was being restricted; not by the producers, but by the requirements of commercial radio. We had to play a large number of advertisements, adhere to certain times and adhere to other rules that are not required by the BBC. In addition, the manager, John Rosborough, had left so I concluded that it was time for me to retire. I had done about twenty-six years in total on radio, so I was ready now to spend more time at home.

Just when I had made the decision to leave, in 2011, I got a call from Eddie West, who is sadly no longer with us. He was the station manager of Downtown Radio, which is where I started back in the seventies. "George, I would love you to come down. If you're thinking of retiring, why don't you do one last year and come back to where you started and complete the circle," he said. I thought that it was a good idea at the time. U105 were not that happy, but I left and went to do a year with Eddie and Downtown Radio. During that year, Eddie became very unwell with cancer. Towards the end of the year, he said, "The show is doing very well, would you stay on for another year?" And I said, "For you, Eddie, yes I will." But, during that second year, because of stress and illness, he had to retire. Another chap came in to replace Eddie and became the station director. He didn't know much about broadcasting, and started to do things that didn't please me. So, I decided there and then, that at the end of that year I would leave. When I left Downtown Radio, in 2013, that was my final goodbye to broadcasting, or so I thought.

On-air at Downtown Radio.

With radio behind me, I carried on with Clubsound, who were now doing a reasonable amount of work. We had money in the bank from our house sale, so Hilary and I decided that maybe it was time that we retired. Then one day, I was walking through the town of Newtownards, and who should come up to me, but Eddie West. I asked him how he was and he said that he had been in remission, but the cancer had since come back. The doctors had controlled it so that it wasn't advancing for now. Being the radio enthusiast that he was, he said, "I've started an Internet radio, called Fever 40. It's situated in a small shopping arcade and we're worldwide on the Internet. Would you make some jingles for us to promote it because you do great voices and you're a popular guy?" I agreed and then he said, "As a matter of fact, would you come down and do a wee show for us?" It had been a while since I had been on Downtown Radio. Now, I don't mean this in a boastful or an egotistical way, but I was stopped almost every day on the street by people who would say, "Why aren't you on the radio anymore? We miss you," and words to that effect. It was lovely to hear and know that people had missed me and I appreciated the support, but I couldn't explain to people why I'd had to leave the BBC, as they wouldn't understand. Anyway, I went down to look at where Eddie had his radio station. It was a little makeshift studio in a shop unit. I had a look around and told Eddie that we could improve it because Internet radio was going to take off eventually. So, I visited a businessman friend, who was very wealthy and interested in radio, and he invested £20,000 into Fever 40. With that, we were able to purchase new studio equipment. I approached the man who owned the shop unit; I knew him very well. He gave us a bigger unit and reduced the rent. We started recruiting people to present on the station to help us improve it. It worked very well, as we weren't drawing a wage from the radio. We were able to use the money that was invested to pay the rent, the telecom line for the Internet and the PRS (Performing Rights Society) that was needed for the music we were playing. I thought that if I was going to be on radio then I might as well be sponsored. So, I approached friends who owned a local bar and restaurant called The Ramble Inn. The owner, John McLarnon, was a wonderful man and dear friend. Sadly, since then he has passed away. He agreed that it was a good idea and they sponsored me for six months. It wasn't a vast amount of money, but it was good to have an income. Eddie West was able to get another two programmes sponsored as well. We were also able to apply for a digital licence which you were allowed to apply for once you were up and running. Even though it was running on a small basis, it was reaching a lot of people around the world. I enjoyed doing it, but then my sponsorship ran out so I told Eddie that I was going to take a break from radio. I said, "If you're able to get another sponsor for my show, then I might be able to come back for another year or you could get somebody else to fill in the slot." I left and the following week, I got a call from the head engineer to say that Eddie had slipped away. When I learnt that Eddie had died, I decided that for me, it was the final chapter. I had been doing this for Eddie, who I respected so much and I thought that this was a sign to finally say that enough was enough. I believe that God had decided that it was enough as well. 2014 was the end of my broadcasting years on radio.

CHAPTER 14

The World Awaits

I feel that I have been very blessed to travel the world through many different opportunities and initiatives. After travelling to Germany at the young age of seventeen, I developed a strong desire to travel and knew that it was going to play an important part in my life.

One of my adventures that led to a lot of travelling, came as a result of one of my favourite hobbies. It started over forty years ago, when I met a guy called Willie Knox, who worked in Ulster Television. He had been chatting about snow skiing and in those days, it was very expensive to go skiing in Europe. Therefore, Willie introduced me to Aviemore in Scotland, on weekend bus runs, which he arranged through UTV. Whenever we visited; however, it was always incredibly cold, and the snow wasn't crisp and dry; it was wet. The dampness got into our bones as we had to queue for up to thirty minutes for the lifts. Then for seven hundred yards, we skied down the slope. Yet, in spite of it all, I really took to it; hook, line and sinker, as did Hilary.

My lifelong friend, Trevor Kelly, Hilary and I, and some other friends then decided to try Europe for the first time. We went to Sauze d'Oulx, a ski resort in Italy. The first difference we noticed was between the snow in Italy and the snow in Scotland. It was not damp; it was dry snow and the sun was out for most of the time.

We skied through the day, and Trevor and I entertained the group at night with our singing and playing. We certainly did have fun, as I still had my L plates on for skiing. On the last day of the week, we decided that the last one down the slope would buy the first round of drinks. Like everyone else, I did not want to be the last one down. So, when we got to the top of the slope, I was determined to go for it way beyond my skiing ability. With that much eagerness to get down, I tumbled, and ripped, I believe, every muscle in my right leg. In the group, there were some medically trained people, so they got me patched up and gave me painkillers. Everyone went to dinner that night, except me. The painkillers must have knocked me out as I fell asleep and was woken later in the evening. The guys brought in a sledge and insisted that I come with them. They lifted me out of bed and onto the sledge, and brought me into the party. I didn't really have a choice. I sat with my leg in the air, in my pyjamas as I played a guitar while everyone else was fully dressed. I must have looked a right ejit. But sure enough, we had a great time, before the team was called to stretcher me off.

The next morning, I was given crutches and tried walking, but the group was eager to get me into a wheelchair to transport me back to the aircraft. Reluctantly, I sat in the wheelchair and the Italian porter came over and said, "I have to take you out to the plane first, Mr Jones." As he started to wheel me to the plane I tried to chat with him. I was preparing myself to get out of the wheelchair as he got to the bottom of the steps of our plane, when he just kept on going. He wheeled me across the airport to an Aeroflot plane, bound for Russia. I tried to get his attention by pointing and waving my arms at him. "No, no, it's that plane over there," I shouted, but he kept wheeling me even faster. I was exhausted from trying to get this Italian man to understand me when he stopped at the bottom of the Russian plane's steps and burst out laughing. Gently, he turned me around and started to wheel me back to our plane. It was then that I spotted Trevor and the rest of our gang at the airport terminal window, roaring their heads off with laughter. They had tipped the guy to pretend to take me to the wrong plane.

On our subsequent skiing trips, people often recognised me and Trevor from back home and persuaded us to give them a song. Hearing that, was like setting a sweet in front of a child and telling them not to eat it. Gladly, we sang and entertained them.

On one of the skiing trips, Trevor, Hilary, me and our family went to stay in a place in Austria, called Finkenberg. It was only close family and friends in our group so when we got to our charming accommodation, the Neuwirt Hotel, we didn't expect to get up and sing. However, when we went into the hotel, I noticed a guitar on the wall. Naturally, I couldn't resist, so I grabbed the guitar off the wall and began to play, and Trevor and I started singing. The owner of the hotel and his wife came out and started clapping. They sat down and started listening as we played Irish songs. That Saturday night in the hotel, we were invited to come to The Fireman's Ball. It was an annual event that was organised by the local fire brigade known as the Feuerwehr. It was attended by all the locals in the village, and an Austrian duo, called the Bergland Duo, provided the music. We were sitting at a table enjoying all the fun, when the owner of the hotel came up to us. "We heard you guys singing and wondered if you would entertain all the people in the village," he said. Reluctantly, Trevor and I got up and borrowed the guitars from the Austrian duo and played four or five songs. Applause erupted. People loved it. Consequently, this led to the owner and his wife inviting us back to play the following year. They offered us a free holiday in the hotel, provided that we played a couple of nights during the week. And that was the start of many years of playing music on skiing holidays.

Another year, Jimmy Black joined us and played his guitar. The three of us set about singing and entertaining the locals, and visiting holidaymakers in the hotel. At that particular party, was a friend of ours, Jill Russell, from Northern Ireland. She worked for a UK skiing company, called Hourmont. They thought that it would be a brilliant idea if we could put a band together and play for all the Northern Ireland people who they would be bringing out once again to Finkenberg, the following year. So, we invited another guy to join us to play the keyboard. Stevie Thomson, made us into a four-piece band. The name that we were christened with was given to us by the Austrian people. They simply called us, The Irish Band. And so, this amazing journey of entertaining and skiing started for real. Hourmont invited us to come the next year to a village called Götzens, near Innsbruck. The band increased to a six-piece, and we were still known as The Irish Band.

When we arrived, our first performance was held in the place where we were staying, the Edelweiss Hotel. Our next show was at a smaller venue, the Sport Café and believe it or not, eighty people were crammed into the café that was only supposed to hold about fifty or sixty people. Not only that, people were also dancing in the street. The Irish Band had become really popular. Before the end of our week's stay, we were asked to go to the neighbouring village called Birgitz, to the Alpin Hotel. We were told to speak to the owner who was called Gunther Kirchmair. It was a long-established hotel, dating back in history and had always been owned by the Kirchmair family. We walked in and spoke to Gunther, and said that we were the band who would perform in his hotel that night. Looking completely bewildered, he said, "Who sent you?" "The skiing company, Hourmont, told us to play to some of the people staying here," I said. At that, he waved his arms about. "Fine, if you want to play, then set up your equipment over there," he said. And he pointed to an area in the large lounge. In those days, we always brought our own equipment with us; but later on, we ended up hiring it. We carried in our equipment and Gunther, who was behind the bar, began to look more and more bewildered. This poor man didn't seem to know anything about us being asked to perform. We began setting up and started to play. It was about eight o'clock and Gunther began gesturing to us to keep the noise down so that we didn't disturb the neighbours. This was fine with us and we lowered the sound. An hour went by and more people began filtering in, so we played a couple more songs and I said to Gunter, "Is this alright?" Reluctantly, he replied, "Yes, but remember to keep it down." Then about thirty more people came in and I looked over at Gunther, who seemed amazed at all these people arriving in his hotel and buying drinks. As I looked at him, he gave me the thumbs-up sign and said it was fine. As we continued playing, more and more people kept arriving and during the break, I went over to Gunther, who by this time was like a child with bright eyes. He couldn't believe the revenue that he was drawing in. "Is the noise, okay?" I asked. "It's fine, it's fine. As a matter of fact, turn it up," he replied. "What about the neighbours?" I asked. Then his exact words were, "To hell with the neighbours. Just play on." By the end of the night, the hotel was jam-packed and we were rocking and rolling until about two o'clock in the morning. I think Gunther was feeling that he had become a millionaire overnight.

This led to an amazing friendship between me and Gunther. He became like a brother. And before we left that week, he said, "Would you be prepared to come and play for me in my hotel for two weeks, every year? I'll pay for the flights and you'll have free accommodation for you and your wives. If you want to bring anyone else with you, then I'll give you a discount." That became the beginning of thirty years of going to the same area. On the tenth year, the local television and news team in Innsbruck had heard about our popularity and they couldn't understand how a band who came from Northern Ireland and had lived amid the Troubles, could bring people who spread so much happiness and fun. We did the television show and explained how our band had come together and had been welcomed back every year since; we even sang on the show for the viewers. They decided to follow us for a whole week with cameras, including up and down the ski slopes.

After fifteen years of visiting and bringing lots of Northern Ireland people to the village, we got a big surprise one night from Gunther and the local council. They decided that they would give us honorary citizenship of the village for all the wonderful business and entertainment that we had brought them over the years. They brought the village brass band to play, and they presented us with special medals and certificates. Then each member from our band was given the baton to conduct the brass band. It was an incredible honour; we felt that we had become citizens of the place we loved.

At that stage, we didn't have a drummer, we only had a drum machine. Then we met a guy called Patrick Cox, who had an Irish name, although he was born in Germany, but lived in Austria. He was a drummer in one of the biggest bands in Austria, Switzerland and Germany. The band was called the Zillertaler Schurzenjagers. This band was really famous in that part of Europe, and it was incredible to meet him. Patrick loved The Irish Band and he loved the songs that we were playing. We played a show in a hotel and he came to visit. He was very good-looking with long flowing blond hair and looked like a typical, heavy metal rocker. He came up at the end and said to me, "Hi, I thought you guys were great. I would love to play drums with you." I had never met the guy and didn't realise that he was famous at the time. So, I replied, "Yeah right okay, if you want." He asked when we were playing next and I told him that we were playing on Wednesday in the Alpin Hotel and forgot all about it. Wednesday arrived, and we were setting up our equipment when Patrick arrived in a van and brought in a fifteen-piece drum kit, which he began to set up. I suddenly realised that I'd invited him, but I'd forgotten to tell the guys. "Guys, I'm really sorry. I don't know what this fella is going to be like, but he's going to play drums with us," I said. Anyway, we were very nice to him but were still unaware that he was famous. It turned out that he knew almost every song that we were playing, and we couldn't believe what an incredible drummer he was.

When the crowd arrived that night, they could not believe that the famous Patrick Cox was playing drums with The Irish Band. When Patrick was with his band, he had been used to playing to 200,000 people in the valley, on an outside broadcast; that's how big they were. We had made a new friend and he became part of The Irish Band, and continued to play with us every year. People used to say, "Are we going to see The Irish Band with the famous Patrick Cox?" This infamous skiing trip with The Irish Band became a regular annual event for many years. It drew people from Northern Ireland, England and America, who would come to join in the fun with The Irish Band. Unbeknown to us at the time, it became a trip where people would meet up with each other, including lads and young women for the first time. We feel very proud that many of these young people from Northern Ireland, Austria and further afield, eventually got married and had families. This was something wonderful that The Irish Band were responsible for, or was it? Ha! Ha! We were invited to play at a few of the weddings, and some were as far away as Sweden. We were also very privileged to play at a wedding at the beautiful Basilica, in Innsbruck. We became so popular in that area; it was like having another family in Austria. It turned out to be an incredible era for us.

Even my son Jason came with us and began skiing when he was in his early twenties. He became great friends with the young Austrian people of his own age. Little did he know, that later on in life he would meet up with one of the girls again and eventually marry her.

Back home in Newtownards, Jason had been very happy working at NTL and then for some particular reason, the company decided to uproot and leave Northern Ireland completely, which shocked us all. As a consequence, Jason was offered a post to go to either England or Scotland, but that was something he didn't want to do. He had another idea and said to me one day, "Dad, will you help me? I'd like to progress with my skiing and go back to Austria." Jason wanted to return to the same village where I spent thirty years skiing, and become a fully qualified ski instructor. At this point, Jason had only worked as a ski instructor on the artificial ski slopes in our country. By this time, Jason was an accomplished skier and I thought that it would be good if he could pass on his knowledge to others. I phoned my friend Gunther Kirchmair, at the Alpin Hotel in Birgitz and as I've mentioned, Gunther had become part of our family. He came to Natalie's wedding. Gunther said immediately, "Send him over, we'll fit him up and sort him out, and he'll be accepted like our own family." So, I asked Jason what he wanted to do with his house and he said, "Just leave it, it's beautiful. I don't know what will happen. I might come back and I always want to have a home here." Consequently, we became the security team for his home and checked on it regularly. I had suggested that he rented it out and he thought that was a great idea because Hilary and I could keep an eye on it. Good old Mum and Dad. I agreed and he packed up his stuff and headed off to a new life in Austria.

We heard from him regularly; he was doing exceptionally well. He attained a high standard and became a fully qualified ski instructor. He phoned home at one stage to tell us that he was working in a place called Lermoos. It was an attractive but small ski resort, which I thought was perfect for him. He had been approached by one of my friends, who I mentioned earlier in the book, Jill Russell. By then she worked for a company called Top Flight who had a hotel catering for school groups in the village. She asked Jason if, as well as being a ski instructor, he'd like to manage this small hotel. Jason jumped at the chance. This turned out to be another progressive step in Jason's life. Not only had he become a top salesman, a top worker in IT call centres, he was now about to become a hotel manager, and this was all without any qualifications.

Hilary and I were really pleased for him and then out of the blue, Jason announced that he had a new Dutch girlfriend. I told Jason that was terrific. By this time he was twenty-eight years old. I asked him how old his girlfriend was and he said she was nineteen. To which I replied, "Jay, is that not a bit young?!" But he assured Hilary and I that he had fallen in love and that her family were great. "If she's from Holland, then why are her family in Austria?" I asked him. "Dad, they're very rich. And they have a second home in Austria where they spend two months each year," he replied. "Well, what does her father do?" "Her Dad has a huge company that builds luxury yachts," he replied. "Jason, she's the one, stay in there." And then I added, "So, are we going to meet this young lady?" Jason promised to bring her home to Northern Ireland for a week and asked if we would set up a few things. Good old Mum and Dad again.

Jason came home with his girlfriend, who was a delightful young woman. However, we still had the impression that she was a little bit young for him. Regardless, we wished them all the best; they had a lovely time and then set off back to Austria. About a month later, Jason announced that he was moving to Holland. We asked why and he said that they were very much in love. His girlfriend was going to go back to university to study hotel management and Jason wanted to live close to her. "But, you've never been to Holland in your life," I said, "Don't worry Dad, I've already applied for a job and I've applied for licenses and I've already applied for an apartment in the village near where she lives." "Gosh, you've done all this?" I was shocked.

Jason soon arrived home to prepare everything and I asked him what he was going to do with his house. He said he'd decided to sell it. I asked if he was sure. He insisted that he'd thought about it a lot and he went ahead and put it on the market. As the housing market was going through a boom period, Jason had a queue of people wanting to look at the house. Unsurprisingly, he sold it and made an immense profit. We were very proud of him. He was then faced with the huge task of packing his car to the hilt with most of his belongings. His Mum went with him to Holland, to help him organise his new apartment and he looked forward to beginning this new chapter of his life. Before they left, he had told us that he and his girlfriend had a bit of an argument, but everything was alright. We asked if he was sure and Jason was certain that once he got over there, it would be all okay. When they reached the village of Roermond, his mother was very happy with his new apartment and loved where he was staying. The two of them went to Ikea and set about buying furniture to make it comfortable. During the time that Hilary was there, she kept asking him about his girlfriend who hadn't phoned him at all. Hilary phoned me because she was getting worried and I wondered if it had been a wise move. Hilary said she didn't know. She came home and was worried that the family who had been so kind to him in Austria had completely disowned him in Holland. So, here was our son, stuck in a foreign country where he didn't know anyone, and he was about to start a new job, which was going to be a challenge in itself. He seemed depressed on the phone, so I suggested to Hilary that I should go out and spend a few days with him, which I did. I took him out for a drink to various pubs and we tried to see if we could find any English people so that Jason could make new friends, as he didn't speak any Dutch. It was coming up to the weekend and towards the end of my stay, but Jason was still depressed as it hadn't quite turned out the way he had hoped. Even though he had wanted to live in Europe, this was not the way he wanted it to be. I had a think. "Why don't you come home, I'll pay for your flight and we can have a chat about it." Jason agreed and we went home. He spent lots of time thinking and then I said to him, "Why don't you go back to Holland on Monday and see how you get on with your job. After that, if you find that it's a dead end, then you're welcome to come back home and live with us. There'll always be a home here for you."

Jason took our advice and went back to Holland, still hoping to hear from his girlfriend. He started his new job and soon began to settle in. He was working for a call centre that handled huge financial accounts. It was called Amro Banking. It was a very responsible position because he had to have complete security clearance to deal with people's accounts that contained millions of pounds. We were still unsure whether he would stay, but by Wednesday, when his company realised that Jason had been working for NTL, he was given a responsible position as supervisor. So, they asked him if he would like to go to Amsterdam to help them set up the new call centre that they were establishing near to where he lived. He phoned me at the end of the week, bubbling with excitement. "You're sounding very happy," I said. "I am Dad. I went to Amsterdam and met a few guys, two of them live in Roermond. One guy, an American, has just broken up with his girlfriend and he wants to move in with me and share the apartment." Finally, Jason had found drinking buddies. His life took on a new meaning. He progressed incredibly well and just the same as when he was at NTL, he soon progressed to a higher level. Time passed, and before long Jason rang to say that he had met a beautiful Dutch woman, who worked for the Dutch lottery, which was in the same building as him. He said that he would like to bring her home. I looked at Hilary, "Here we go again," I said. Jason is six feet two, and when we met his girlfriend, we couldn't believe that she was the same height as him. Melanie was a beautiful girl, and you could see in her and Jason's eyes that their love was real.

Before long, Jason's American friend moved out of the apartment and Melanie moved in. They seemed to get on very well and by the end of the year, Jason asked if I would ring our friend, Steve Knight in New York, who I had met on the cruises. I asked Steve if Jason and Melanie could come and stay with him as Melanie wanted to visit New York. In New Jersey style, Steve replied, "Yeah sure, send them over. They're going to be part of the family." So, they both set off for New York, but what we didn't know was that while he was there, Jason asked Steve if he could go out with him and choose a ring. He had planned to propose to her in Central Park. He got down on one knee before Melanie. He sent us photographs that looked very romantic. Hilary and I thought, 'Wow, another wedding is in the offing." Melanie's family wanted to have the wedding here in Northern Ireland, so we planned, not an Irish wedding, but a Scottish wedding. The reason for this was that both my family and Hilary's had a very strong Scottish influence. My grandmother, as I mentioned earlier, was born in Clydebank in Scotland. In addition, my grandfather had strong Scottish connections; his name was McConnell, which was my mother's maiden name. Hilary's father's name was Roy, so therefore there was a very strong Scottish connection. We applied for McConnell tartan kilts and ties for the wedding, which made Jason very proud. My two granddaughters were flower girls and they both had Roy tartan sashes in a highland style around their shoulders. We also had the world champion piper, Robbie Watt, who had won the championship five times over. He agreed to play the pipes as the bride walked down the aisle and pipe the bride and bridegroom out of the church after the wedding ceremony. Robbie was a very dear friend, who believe it or not, now lives in the same village in Austria as Jason. Robbie was another person who I introduced to skiing, which could have had something to do with it.

Before the wedding, which wasn't until later in the year, we got a call from Jason who said, "Dad, hold onto your hat, you're going to be a grandfather." On 24 January 2008, we celebrated the birth of our wonderful grandson, Ethan. "Thank goodness that the Jones clan is going to continue," I said to myself quietly.

Jason and Melanie were happily married for eleven years and Ethan grew up to be a lovely young boy and we were very proud of him. Sadly, it wasn't to last and Jason and Melanie went their separate ways. Jason was very dismayed but realised that it had to be. Hilary and I were aware that something had been bubbling for some time, so we almost knew before Jason rang to confirm our fears. Not only were we sad for Jason, but we feared that we could be deprived of seeing our grandson. Fortunately, Melanie assured us that we were Ethan's grandparents and we were welcome to see him at any time and that she would even bring him to Northern Ireland.

Jason was very sad about the break-up, so we encouraged him to come and stay with us for a while. When he arrived, he explained that he was happy to stay in Holland as he had a good job and a good home. He became the sole owner of the house when Melanie moved out. However, we were concerned that he would become lonely, so I invited him to come skiing with us. I reminded him how he enjoyed listening to The Irish Band when he was growing up and that he had made many friends over the years. Jason agreed and when he arrived, he soon reunited with his friends and had a wonderful time. One of the girls who he met up with, was a young woman who he had always got on well with. Her name was Kathrina Hoffer, although she was known as Kat. Suddenly, Kat who worked for Austrian airlines as a senior air stewardess, started travelling to Holland. Likewise, Jason began travelling to Austria. Although this time it was not for skiing, it was just to be with Kat. I realised that God had put these two people together now for a purpose, after all this time.

After a couple of years, Jason came home. "Mum, I've bought an engagement ring. I'm sending it to you and I want you to bring it on the next skiing holiday. I don't want Kat to find it." So, it was all arranged and everyone else knew about the proposal. Me, Hilary, Jason, Kat and one of Kat's best friends, Cathy, who was affectionately known as Noodle, went to the top of the mountain. Kat had no idea whatsoever what was going on. The five of us stopped on the top of the mountain for a break, to catch our breath before we went down. Kat was admiring the scenery when suddenly Jason walked to her side, took off his ski helmet, got down on one knee and produced the ring that we had brought with us. Kat was absolutely shocked and she fell backwards onto the snow. Jason knelt beside her and asked, "Is it yes?" And she said, "Of course it's yes." We skied back to one of the restaurant bars, where there were about sixty people waiting. Unbeknown to Kat, I had previously told everyone that if I had my right hand up, it was a yes and if my left hand was up, it was a no; so that they knew exactly how to react. As we skied down, I put up my right hand and everyone cheered. Kat was overjoyed and we celebrated with champagne.

* * *

Another way that music opened up travel for my wife and I, was through a friend called Alan Couser. Alan worked for a well-known travel company and was head of the cruise department. He said to me one day, "George, I have heard that you take a band skiing, to entertain people. I book a lot of people onto cruises from Northern Ireland. Would you and your band like to come with your wives, at my invitation to play on a cruise to entertain the Northern Ireland folk?" I agreed that it would be a lovely idea. But I never suspected that I was about to embark on another long adventure of travelling and playing music. Only this time, it would not be in the Austrian Alps, it would be on the ocean waves.

Alan made me an offer that I couldn't refuse. "This would be the deal, if you can put a band together, I can get you on to the QE2 ship to perform. The ship will be going from Southampton to New York, on a transatlantic cruise," Alan said. I asked what was included. "We'll give you free flights to Southampton, entrance onto the QE2, free cabins and free food. You can bring your wives and do three performances on the eight-day crossing," Alan replied. This sounded too good to be true.

Trevor agreed that this could be done and we modified The Irish Band that had grown to seven people down to a five piece, and renamed it, Emerald Connection. We started rehearsing for the QE2 and when we realised that people would be coming from all over for this cruise and wanting to be entertained at night, we learnt additional music. We mixed *Danny Boy, Fields of Athenry, Wild Rover* and good old Irish folk songs with Clancy Brothers' songs. We also performed an Andrew Lloyd Webber tribute show, A Barbershop Quartet and we did a Latin American medley of wonderful songs as we expected that there would be Spanish-speaking and South American travellers. Consequently, we assured ourselves that we had covered all the bases and could be regarded as an international band.

I had never been on a cruise ship and the QE2 was my first cruise; it would set the bar high. I was familiar to some degree of the history of this famous ship and I had heard of Hollywood stars who had travelled on it. But when we arrived at the QE2 after the flight, I was mesmerised with the size and the eloquence of it. It was glamour with a capital G.

We got settled in and Alan came and said, "I have one of the bars booked for the Northern Ireland people and we're going to have a *sail-away party.* Will you play at it, as one of your first gigs?" The bars and theatres all had their own sound equipment that we would need because there were about five bands playing throughout the trip, on different sets.

That night as the ship sailed, we entered the bar and you have probably heard about Northern Ireland folk in bars. When they saw us coming in, they recognised us and the shouts and roars erupted; you would have thought that we were famous stars. Because of the dancing and the crowd attendance, the main doors were left open. Suddenly, non-

Northern Ireland people were queuing to get in; they had seen how the Northern Irish folks entertained themselves. The Irish are world famous because of the Irish bars around the world. Regardless of how joyful people were, fights were uncommon, and so people knew they were in a safe environment. We played in the Golden Lion Pub, which was situated on one of the decks of the ship, and we regularly had full houses even though it was only in the afternoon. Then the ship's entertainment officer heard about this and asked if we would move to a larger event in the evenings and bring our crowd with us which, of course, we did.

At the end of the week, everything we had done proved a success for them and in turn, we suggested that as we were a cabaret band, we could put on a cabaret show in their theatre. They said no, because it was booked up and the big review show was on twice a night. There was just no time to fit us in. But they could let do a midnight show. But it would be a chance that we would have to take, as people were going to bed for the next day's venture. But they agreed to advertise it."

We agreed to give it a shot on the last day before we disembarked in New York, and dressed up in our cabaret suits. All glammed up and set to do a one-hour show, we took a chance, hoping that at least some people who had heard us on the voyage would turn out for it. Thankfully, the theatre was packed and when the show ended, everyone stood up and gave us a standing ovation, not once but twice. Pat Murphy, who was the resident comedian at the theatre, came over and said, "I've been the resident compere on this ship for twenty-five years and no one has ever received a standing ovation." Suddenly, all the guys including me, went from being five feet tall to feeling over eight feet tall.

The ship's senior management, Cunard, contacted Alan and asked if we would come back next year. Of course, we agreed and when we returned home, I went to Ian Kennedy and suggested that this would make a good documentary. We could show people around the ship and what it was like to be on a cruise. Ian went to the BBC, and they agreed that they would get behind the making of this one-off programme.

The following year we set sail again, only this time there was a BBC film crew with us to film, *George and the Queen*. At nights, we played in the theatre, and during the day we were filming for the BBC. I believe I was in every nook and cranny on that ship following the film crew or they were following me, just to tell a story. Their kitchen was incredible; they had fifteen chefs and the head chef was Austrian. There were different types of freezer rooms for all varieties of food. They had two special rooms that were dedicated to housing different types of caviar. There were rooms for different champagnes and wines, and so on. When I saw the magnitude of the food, I realised what their motto meant, *There's nothing on this ship that you can ask for that we have not got.* They catered for everyone.

George and the Queen invite.

As we walked down a section of the ship, which was called the Hall of Fame, we saw pictures of Charlie Chaplin, Laurel and Hardy, Clarke

Gable, Humphrey Bogart, among many others; They had all had travelled on the QE2.

We interviewed a lady and her little dog. Before her husband passed away, his bequest to her was that she could stay on the ship for the rest of her life. The only condition was that she could only be a guest on the ship for eleven months of the year, because in the remaining month, the ship goes in to dry dock to be serviced. They even had a luxury section on the lower decks of the ship, that was reserved for people's pets. They were treated like royalty, just like the guests.

I had the privilege of steering the ship, but whether it was faith or fear that the captain was operating under, he would only give me the wheel when we were in the middle of the Atlantic Ocean. And that was only after he had checked all angles of the ocean, in case I might hit something. I was impressed with being behind the wheel and getting to see what the captain sees, until they took me up to their two, first-class, executive lounges. That's when I became really impressed. Each suite had its own restaurant; imagine that. If I hadn't seen it, I would never have believed it. The whole purpose of this was so that VIPs would never have to meet with anyone else on board the ship. These were for famous people such as David Bowie, Elton John, and so on. Furthermore, if you didn't like flying, this was not just a room with a view, but almost like having your own hotel. I found out that when the ship goes for its around-the-world cruise, an American lawyer books these two suites; one for his family and another for a family close to them. The money he paid for these suites covered the price of the fuel for an around-the-world trip. I would like to become acquainted with this man; especially now with the price of fuel.

During the first trip that we took on the QE2 in April 2001, we visited *The Windows on the World* at the top of the Twin Towers, where we enjoyed a meal. But the difference between that cruise and this second one the following year, was that 9/11 had taken place.

The ship normally arrived in New York at dawn, and came up the Hudson River with the Statue of Liberty on the left. People got out of their beds and saw that lovely morning view. But this visit was different; no one was allowed on deck because of the security risk; even to do a commentary was a risk in the national securities' eyes. I explained to the captain that this documentary was mainly for Northern Ireland and to express its sympathy from the Northern Ireland people towards the people of New York. On hearing this, he said, "When the ship comes through the outer markers on the Hudson River, two mini-submarines will tail us, armed helicopters will hover over the ship, and armed coastguard will be landing on the ship because we are in a red-alert stage in case another attack happens. Armed guards will be on every section of the ship and absolutely no passengers will be allowed outside on the decks." He then said, "You will be allowed outside to film for ten minutes and then you must come back in." If I remember rightly, my opening line was, "Here we are on the deck of the QE2 as it comes up the Hudson River approaching New York, with the famous Statue of Liberty and its skyline. But as you know by now, that iconic skyline has changed with the absence of the Twin Towers, much to the sadness of America." Here I was, trying to paint a picture of what was missing on the skyline, and in the back of my mind, I was thinking about the previous year, when we were sitting at the top of the Twin Towers in that restaurant.

What my cameraman didn't capture in the shot was a six-foot tall, armed American coastguard officer, standing beside me armed to the teeth and wearing a flak jacket as he waited in case anything unusual took place. Because the officer was on duty, he never looked at us but continued looking straightahead. When I finished my speech for Northern Ireland out of sympathy for New York, he still didn't look at me, but he said out of the side of his mouth, "Hi kid, my folks were Irish, and what you said there was great and I shed a tear. You did good kid." What he didn't realise, was that I was probably a lot older than him.

After we had finished cruising on the QE2, we took a break for a year. We were then approached by Alan Couser again, who invited us to perform on the Royal Caribbean ships. This became the start of another journey of cruising and performing, with our band, Emerald Connection, around the Mediterranean. We did our usual performance, but the purpose was to entertain the Northern Ireland contingent. Therefore, we weren't paid; we were just given a free holiday. We met the entertainment director, who had heard of our exploits on the QE2, and we were told that we'd only be required to play three times on the ten-day cruise. We proceeded to play at the first venue, which was not a very large room, but the people piled in. Word soon got around about our performance and it became clear that we would need a larger venue. Hence, we were given Cleopatra's room, which was a huge ballroom that held about eight hundred people. It was adorned with a sphinx and decorated with Egyptian decor and artefacts. So, we decided to go and listen to the band that was playing the night before us. They were resident on the ship and travelled for months at a time. This band, which was from America, played to about one hundred people. They were an absolutely amazing band, but what we noticed straightaway was that they had no contact with the crowd. They hardly spoke to the people; they just played songs. It was like a brick wall between them and the crowd. They looked totally devoid of enthusiasm as no doubt you would be, if you were playing every night for ten weeks. Nevertheless, we hoped we'd get a crowd the next night because it would be demoralising to play to only one hundred people in a room that holds eight hundred. So, we arrived the next night and to our amazement, the place was packed. Again, our band started to enjoy success on a different cruise line. Two of the American guys from the other band came up to us at the end of the night and said, "Would you guys like to come and do a two-band show with us later on in the cruise?" They wanted us to play with them so that they could play to a crowd. Unfortunately, we couldn't as there were restrictions and we were told where to play and when not to play.

We cruised every year for four years on the Royal Caribbean. They were beautiful ships, but they were actually cruise ships, rather than the QE2, which was an ocean liner. What saddened us the most, was that every year, the ships seemed to get a lot bigger, therefore the crowds got bigger, which became too claustrophobic. The last one that we travelled on held a total of nearly four thousand people. It was like a floating holiday camp and I didn't like that amount of people and from what I gather nowadays, they are even larger than that. Where's it all going to end? Sadly though, it didn't have the same atmosphere as the QE2 and the smaller ships.

On our last cruise, we heard that the ship had been damaged in the dock coming in to Southampton; therefore, she had to wait for repairs. As a consequence, we flew out to the Mediterranean and joined the ship there. When the time came for the ship to dock in Barcelona, a huge storm had arrived. As a result, the people began to panic. The temporary repairs on the ship had not been finished properly, and the windows were blown out by the storm and water was coming onto the ship. The crew did seem to be on top of it and were in control, but as word spread around the ship, the people became panicky. We had all our gear packed up as we were going to fly home once we'd docked in Barcelona. However, the entertainment director came to us and said, "Guys, would you do me a big favour? Could you please play us an afternoon concert, until we can dock the ship? We need to keep the people calm." We played for two hours to a massive crowd. They had chosen to ask us out of all the resident bands. It was difficult to play because the ship was swaying and the microphone stands were slipping from one side of the stage to the other. But being typically Irish, we gritted our teeth and ended up receiving a standing ovation. The director said, "Look, anytime you guys want to come on the ship, that would be wonderful." But the problem was that they were too enthusiastic about getting us onto the ship. They rang Alan Couser and said, "We would like to have them on board but they're far too good to be on for two weeks or ten days, so would the guys like to come on for ten weeks?"

Unfortunately, we had to say no because we all had jobs. For the first time in our lives, we were turned down because we were far too good.

We made an album featuring some of the favourite songs that people had enjoyed on their cruises. It was called *Emerald Connection at Sea or Whatever Floats Your Boat.* That was another achievement that has blessed me in my recording career.

CHAPTER 15

Do You Come Here Often?

Travelling in connection with music and broadcasting has been incredible and opened up a whole new world for me throughout my life. I've now been playing the guitar for sixty-six years. I've spent over fifty years playing with Clubsound, thirty-five years in broadcasting, thirty years skiing, and twenty-one years producing a legendary theatre show called, *Do You Come Here Often?* More recently, I have spent five years producing a show called, *The Rock 'n' Roll Years and Dance Hall Days.* If you count those up, you'll probably be astounded by the fact that I'm not over two hundred years old.

The theatre show, *Do You Come Here Often?,* was an incredible success and it began on my radio show on the BBC when I decided one day that I would devote the whole show to the legendary showbands of Ireland. These showbands were part of Irish history. At one time, there were almost eight hundred showbands on the road in Ireland. As a matter of fact, Ireland had its own pop charts and its own pop stars. As I mentioned earlier in the book, the primary pastime of people in the late fifties and sixties was dancing, so therefore, there was a dance hall in nearly every town and village in Northern Ireland. When they provided the entertainment, the showbands became massively popular. I have to mention here, that no dance hall was allowed to sell alcohol. If you wanted a drink, then you had to have one before you went in. Sometimes the doormen would smell your breath and if they could smell beer, then they wouldn't let you in; that's how strict it was. But in Northern Ireland, sadly this came to an end because of the Troubles. So, on this particular day on my radio show, I decided to play music by these famous bands. I thought that it would bring back some wonderful memories of when the people enjoyed their dancing years. Little did I know that it would spark off this incredible show, and I found it difficult because I had very little recorded material from the showbands; just a few CDs. On that day the phones didn't stop ringing for two hours. People were calling up to say how much they loved these memories and that it took them back to their youth. I thought this was a great idea, so two months later, I tried it out again for two hours on my show, and to my amazement, there were calls from showband members who were still playing the music from that beloved era. After hearing all these wonderful stories from these showband guys, I thought that this would make a brilliant stage show. So, I went to my dear friend David Hull, who had been my agent for years, and said, "Because of the Troubles, the showband years were cut short for these people who loved to dance and listen to them. So, why don't we bring it back for them as a stage show and find out how many showband stars there are in Ireland who are still around?" He thought that it was a great idea and we decided to experiment.

In the springtime of 1991, we did one show at the famous Waterfront Hall in Belfast. The show was an instant sell-out and when I say sell-out, it held two thousand five hundred people. This was also made up of the choir seats that were behind the stage and we even filled them. This meant that they were looking at our backs, but they didn't seem to mind. It made us realise how much people had longed for these happy times to come back again and we were giving them just a little taste of the memories they still had. We thought this through and my agent David Hull said that he would book another two nights in the autumn. To our astonishment, the show sold out again almost as soon as the tickets went on sale.

It became an annual event that grew in popularity and lasted for over two decades. BBC Northern Ireland Television recorded three of these shows and they were put out as a feature programme every year, while in their year book, they said that this was the most singularly watched programme of the year. The number of our performances increased, and more and more showband stars were found. Many of the stars were living around the world, including one of the big stars at the time, Brendan Bowyer, who we coaxed to come out of retirement in Las Vegas; and he came back many times to Northern Ireland just to appear on the show over the next twenty-one years. They were happy to re-live their youth, even if it was just for one night. This particular show still holds the record in the Waterfront Hall that was sold out for eight nights in a row to just over two thousand people per night. What I believe I did with this idea, was to help people once again re-live their past and forget about the Troubles; and also remind them how it was in the trouble-free years. Was God telling me to do this through the radio show, I wonder? This was something else that God had possibly motivated me to do; to bring enjoyment to the people. In one sense, we had defeated the Troubles and brought the people full-circle, by bringing the stars back for them.

The showband shows were coming to an end, because a lot of the great stars and names who the crowd associated with, were passing away. Me and David Hull decided to call it a day with the showband shows because sadly, a lot of the great stars were passing away and we only wanted to put on a proper show with the original stars. During the last three years, I produced another show of memories with David Hull called, *The Rock 'n' Roll Years* and *Dance Hall Days*. It was an idea that came to me with Clubsound as the main band and with four wonderful singers — Hoe Mac, Trevor Kelly, Janet McCartney and Catherine McCallum. We paid tribute to the amazing stars from the fifties and sixties. I read out the biography of these great stars and these singers came out in turn, and sang three hits from that particular star.

This show ran for about three years and when the showband shows finally came to an end, I asked David about how we could replace it. He said, "Why don't we upgrade your other show, *The Rock 'n' Roll Years and Dance Hall Days*, and perform it at the Waterfront Hall and the large theatres where the showband shows once performed. But I want to add something different to it." So, I contacted a dear friend, Roy Heybeard, who had been a great artistic director in the Arts Theatre in Belfast. He had been known for producing and directing great musical shows. He was in retirement, but when I approached him with the idea, he was very enthusiastic. I provided all the musical details and the stars who would feature in the show and left it with him. Before long and after a few meetings, we had come up with not just a concert, but a musical with drama. It was based on the idea that I would be an agent on one side of the stage in my office with appropriate scenery and the other side would be a coffee bar. My role would be to discover all these people who were later to become stars. For example, Cliff Richard, whose real name was Harry Webb, I would rename Cliff Richard and acting as an agent, I would do the same with Dusty Springfield and Patsy Cline, to name but a few. For the last five years, we toured around the theatres in Ireland with the show. It was a great success. Another satisfaction for me was when I looked around at the audience, who were mainly the older generation, and they had that *look* in their eye when they remembered each and every song, and each and every star of the music that sadly we don't hear on the radio anymore. However, it brought them joy once again just for one night and they told us so.

CHAPTER 16

When You've Tried Everything

At the age of seventy, I became very disillusioned with my life. I didn't feel like a pensioner, I felt very young at heart. I wanted to do a lot more with my life but there were no outlets and I didn't feel that I had many options or opportunities left to pursue. It was as though the world was going round again; I didn't want to have to get a job stacking shelves or working in a factory. Not that I didn't want to do it, but if I did, it would have been the same as when I was working at the vacuum cleaner company. I have come to realise, that if you have a job that is in the limelight, then people think that you're instantly a millionaire, but this is simply not so. People think that you're worth a fortune, but it doesn't work like that. Consequently, I drifted into a period that was verging on depression and verging on a state of not knowing what to do with myself. The telephone had also stopped ringing, which was another sign that I wasn't required anymore. And then you begin to realise that because of your age, you could be too old for broadcasting and stage work and I'm sure that a lot of my colleagues in the business have felt this way, at some point. Gradually, I fell into a void and didn't know which direction to go in for the latter part of my life.

As I reflected on my life, I realised that I had travelled the world, hosted the royalty of showbiz, interviewed heads of states, and been given the best tables in restaurants; instead of me being thankful for such a life, here was I sinking deeper into this void. I am sure like many who will read this book and have moved into the retirement stage of life, the feeling of being an unwanted gift comes to mind.

Depression started to set in although Hilary gave me great encouragement, it was my daughter, Natalie, who shone the light onto my darkness.

I had always watched my daughter and been aware of her faith in God, as he helped her face the many challenges in her life with her eyesight. In 2015, she introduced me to Christianity, which became a stabilizer. Natalie and her husband Jeff, have been Christians for a long time and have firm connections with their church; which is the one that they were married in.

I remember the day that Natalie encouraged me with Christianity. "Dad, if you've tried everything for your depression, why don't you try God? Just come to church and tell God about your problems and what you're going through," she said. Hilary and I went to the church that Natalie and Jeff attended, which was the First Presbyterian Church in Bangor. I spent many weeks listening to our minister and listening to people talk about their faith. My wife and I felt inspired and suddenly light began to filter into our lives and extinguish the darkness. A church member came up to me one day. "You know, God has touched you in your life, whether you know it or not," he said. That was when I began to realise that everything I had in my life was from God and that my talents of playing music, broadcasting and entertaining people were not self-created, but gifts from God. It was not me who dreamt up these gifts and ideas inside me, it was the Maker Himself who created them. For each one of us, we must discover the gifts that have been given to us. I am so grateful to God for the many gifts that He has blessed me with and I realise that I had never thanked Him for it.

After that revelation, I knew in my heart that I had to commit to a purpose in life. I realised that this was the path that I wanted to take and that God wanted me to take. I also began to realise that God had a plan and a journey for me, and had blessed me with these gifts. In the spring of 2015, I accepted Jesus Christ as Lord of my life and invited him into my heart. Oh, how my life changed. Through God I have found internal peace, contentment and absence from depression. This is what I had been desperately seeking in the darkness and the void that had begun to take root in my life. When people found out that I had become a Christian and I was still involved in the world of showbiz and entertainment, they began to question whether I would change or not. They were puzzled, and wondered whether it would last and would I be any different? I assured them that my performance would be exactly the same; the only difference was that I had God inside me. On top of that, I wasn't prepared to preach to people that they had to become a Christian. I was still going to be the George Jones that they knew. Even standing on stage at my age, when I can say that it's not as easy as it used to be as a young rock 'n' roller, I say a prayer before I go on. I ask God to help me to continue to entertain the audience into the night. My prayer is always answered. God is so gracious and faithful, and enables me to keep going all these years with the many talents that He has so generously blessed me with.

Right now, I walk with a sense of calmness and a caring for my fellow man. I have always cared for people, but now that God lives in me, my concern for people runs deeper. I also believe that God has gifted me to care for people through the talents that I have received.

During the Covid years, it was God's strength that gave me and my family the ability to cope, as I'm sure that He did with many families. It was during this time that I discovered another gift that God had given to me. It started five years ago, when my sister came to tell me that she was clearing stuff from the house after her beloved husband, Billy, had died. She found an old brown envelope that she had kept. Remember I said earlier that my sister kept everything, But I had no idea what was inside. I opened it and found sketches that I had done when I was thirteen years old. It was an amazing discovery. I suddenly remembered that I had, in fact, studied art through a correspondence course for one year and I had forgotten all about it. This prompted me to find my paints and I began painting the old sketches that Lally had found. This led to me buying more paints and art material. All of a sudden, I found myself journeying in another direction that was away from entertainment, broadcasting and everything else, and into the world of art. It was a perfect antidote to the depression that Covid lockdown had caused. In the very early stages, I often told myself that I couldn't draw or paint. However, when I finished my first painting, I was just as astonished as my family by what I had created and I realised that this was another talent from God that enabled me to do this. As the number of my paintings increased, people wanted these pictures to put in their homes. I painted landscapes, landmarks, animals, favourite pets, and anything else that reminded people of their memories. I felt that God was giving me something else with which to bless others.

Art is another remarkable venture in my life, motivated I believe by God when Lally, brought me that brown envelope. Now, when I attempt commissions for people; painting their dreams, visions or memories; I always say a prayer before I start painting, and ask God for his help, because sometimes I think that the task is too much for me. However, when the painting is complete, I am astonished when I look at it. "I couldn't have done that without God's help," I say. During the last two or three years, I have completed over two hundred paintings.

When I was in church, I always sat upon the dais because I also played bass guitar in the worship band. During the sermon, images came to me and I sketched them on the back of the music paper. After a couple of Sundays, the minister realised what I was doing and she said to the congregation, "If you think that George is being ignorant and not listening to the sermon, he's not, he's drawing prophetic art messages that he has been given from God." During the week, I often received messages from God of images to draw for the coming Sunday. These turned out to be prophetic messages for other people. In addition, thoughts came to me and I painted them, only to then find out on Sunday that the message from the minister was what I had painted. I'm totally in awe of how God does this.

I have completed a folder of sketches that I painted during the years that I was at First Presbyterian Church, Bangor. I do accept thanks from people, but I know deep down that it is God working through me when I paint. From prophetic paintings to commissioned paintings, if you drive past our home, even after midnight, the light will be on and you'll see me sitting at the end of our large dining table, much to my wife's dismay, while I paint the next picture and marvel at God's grace.

God has blessed me with good health so that I can continue playing music to entertain people, but even though I have an artificial knee because of thirty years of skiing. Ha! Ha! When I am no longer able to perform, He has ensured that I still have another talent in my life to pursue. I enjoy providing happiness for people by painting for them. While I am still able-bodied and I continue to hear from God, even in old age, then I will continue to paint many more pictures. Although I'm not going to become Vincent Van Gogh and cut off my ear, because if I'm going to keep on playing music, then I will need both of them.

I'm not sure if God has anything else in store for me, but one thing I do know, is that His plans are good, and because of that I will bow to Him at all times. Everything that we have is from God. I am becoming more and more aware of how I have been motivated by God throughout my life; as a consequence, all I want to do is inspire other people.

I encourage you now to look back on your life and start thanking God for the blessings He has given you, circumstances that you might have thought were inconsequential and affected you, but recognise that God had a hand in it.

CHAPTER 17

A Tribute to Family and Friends

You have followed my journey through life and heard of my ups and downs, the periods when we have been down and out, the periods when we have climbed back up again, got through health problems, and various other disappointments in our lives; now is the part that I want to tell you about the people who have helped, encouraged and supported me. Although I realise that God has guided me, even when I wasn't aware of it, I believe that God put certain people in the right place, at the right time to strengthen me — first of all, my family.

As a matter of fact, while writing this book with my good friend Jennifer, from Maurice Wylie Media editorial team, who has helped me so much with this story, we discovered these moments that had an effect on my life which we affectionately called *God moments*.

My amazing first lady, Hilary

This lady and I have now been married for fifty-three years and I can honestly say that I am so blessed to have such a wonderful woman in my life. We got married in 1969 and in the years that followed, she has stuck by me through thick and thin. She has travelled the world with me unselfishly, knowing that I wanted to become a star — that was my driving force. I didn't know until lately that it created a void that only God can fulfil.

The lady of my life — Hilary.

Hilary sacrificed everything that she had wanted to do in those early years, and became a devoted wife and mother. Next to God, I owe most of my life to her and could never repay her. Hilary is a brave and independent woman, and in the last ten to fifteen years, she has proved that even more. Through her great love of animals, especially horses, she has blossomed into an incredible riding instructor. Through God's guidance and His close relationship with Hilary, He has gifted her to teach horse riding to special needs and physically challenged children. This all started thirty years ago when she joined an organisation called RDA (Riding for the Disabled Association). She became an instructor for the association and then went on to become a county coach. For many years, she devoted a lot of time to travelling and teaching the

RDA group. In 2016, she realised the need for a private RDA group. The RDA schools are set up to work through special schools. When these children are released from school at the end of the day, they are taken on a bus to a riding school and given an hour of tuition by instructors such as Hilary. So, Hilary decided with the encouragement of Natalie and me, to set up a private RDA group here at our home. It was known as the Ballyboley group. Hilary's main reason for doing this was to give special needs adults and children the opportunity to learn to ride. While Hilary teaches the children, the parents have time to sit down and have a cup of tea in the small wooden shed that we built. What has amazed us, is how the children become so settled in the company of the horses. They benefit both physically and psychology from riding. When it started, it was amazing because we were able to see the joy on the parent's faces and sometimes we saw tears in their eyes as Hilary attained great standards of riding with these children. It was definitely a moment when we were aware of God's presence in our home, as He helped Hilary to do this. Natalie and I both believed that this was another gift from God. Hilary has always maintained a humble attitude when lots of grateful thanks and appreciations have been bestowed upon her, but I know exactly what she has done in this world, especially for special needs children over the last six years. If it was up to me, I would award her an MBE, but that's because I love her so much. We have always been very proud of Hilary; she is a great mother and in the latter years has been a magnificent grandmother. I don't think that I could have wished for a more wonderful partner to stand beside me through this journey. And now the two of us are standing beside each other in God's light — you can't beat it.

My wonderful son Jason: I am incredibly proud of him

Jason has always been precious to Hilary and me, especially after what happened when we took him to South Africa. He has maintained an independent attitude since he was very small, for which I love him. At times, I have thought that he is like a carbon copy of me because he didn't enjoy school, but on the other hand, even though he loved his music he never took up an instrument, until later in life. This turned out to be his love for drumming and he bought himself a drumkit. He practised furiously and in all the homes that he has lived in, there has always been a drumkit.

George and his son Jason and grandson Ethan.

Jason and our daughter-in-law, Kat, now live in Austria. Our grandson lives in Holland and we have watched him grow up, and see him often. Ethan, who will soon be fifteen, has grown up to be a wonderful young man. He spends all of his vacations with his dad and he travels to Northern Ireland to spend Christmas with us. That side of our family is now complete and they are all doing wonderfully well.

My beautiful daughter Natalie, who has been an inspiration to us

My daughter Natalie, lives next door to Hilary and me, with her husband Jeff and their two daughters. Throughout Natalie's life, she has always amazed us. Although it has been necessary for us to give her our support, she has unknowingly supported us through her strength in God — she taught us.

From left: George and Hilary's granddaughter Sophie,

daughter Natalie and granddaughter Jessie.

Natalie has two beautiful daughters; Sophie and Jessica. They are both Christian girls and she has guided them throughout their lives. Jessica, at eighteen, is a trainee paramedic and Sophie, at twenty, is working as cabin crew for Aer Lingus and has an ambition to become a pilot. Jeff has been a wonderful husband to Natalie, and assisted her at all times when she has needed him. He reminds me of Natalie's Uncle Billy, who could turn his hand to anything. Jeff is a practical man and understands the mechanics of machinery, including power engines. In the latter stages of our lives, Hilary and I have always turned to Jeff for help with all our practical needs and he has been a great son-in-law.

George's beloved sister Lally

There's just not enough thanks to bestow upon the person I love as much as my dear sister, Lally. As you will know from reading this book, she started introducing me to the world of music at a very early age. I don't think that there is a person in this world who could have had a better older sister than me. In the latter years of my life, she became more like a maternal figure, a second mother if you will; not just to me, but to Hilary and my entire family. She has guided us through many, many things and as you've read in this book, has touched us with God's help. She is now a resident in a care home in Northern Ireland, where I visit her regularly. She has a wonderful daughter, Audrey, who cares for her mother and visits her several times a week. Lally also has a son, Stephen, who is very similar to his father Billy; he is a quiet man. Her niece and nephew love her just as much as I do. She is still beautiful to me, even at the age of eighty-seven. She still tries very hard to be that vibrant, happy, funny person who I've known all my life, but sadly the horrible disease of dementia has set in. As the months go by, I keep losing a little bit of my beloved Lally. But I know that many families have to face up to this just as I have, but each time I see her, I remember her exactly the way I first saw her when I was growing up as a child and she will always remain so. And I know when the time comes, that God will take care of her and reunite her with her beloved Billy.

George and his sister Lally meeting up after a show at the Waterfront.

These are people who I would like to thank — my dear friends

I would like to go back to where it all began and give a special thank you to my school chums who later became The Monarchs. Billy McAllen, in particular, was my best friend during my school years and teenage life. He was a shy person but an amazing guitar player. We had wonderful times together.

Then Roy Kane came along and became our drummer. He is a flamboyant, outspoken person who I love to bits because he says it the way it is.

Wesley Black, who I also mentioned earlier, was an incredible piano player. I am saddened that Wesley was taken far too early in life by terrorists.

Van Morrison, who at an early stage, became a dear friend and he still is today. And even though he has become one of the world's mega stars in the world of music and writing, he still finds time to go back to his roots and remember the people such as me, Billy and Roy, and where it all started. We often have lunch together, and reminisce about the incredible times of our youth. I will always continue to wish him the best in his career and I'm proud to have started off in early life, sharing our musical lives together.

The Monarchs as they are today.

From left: Roy Kane, George Jones, Harry Mac, Van Morrison and Billy McAllen.

My best friend of all time for over fifty years, is Trevor Kelly. In some respects, I would rate Trevor as being the brother I never had. We have shared the most incredible experiences and adventures in life, not just through friendship, but also through music. Trevor and I have sung together and performed in some of the most incredible places around the world. I value his friendship as a gift from God.

I never had any brothers, just one wonderful sister, although as I have just mentioned, Trevor Kelly was the closest I've had to a brother. However, I do claim to have known four men who have stuck by me through the majority of my musical career. And I think that qualifies them to be regarded as my four brothers, which is what I call them. When you work with someone for fifty years, I believe that you have a licence to call them your brother. I couldn't ask for four more wonderful guys to work with, and that, of course, is my Clubsound family.

The first one I have to mention is drummer, David McKnight. Like me he was one of the original founders of Clubsound. Davy and I have known each other for fifty-plus years. As a matter of fact, we're very much alike and people often mistook us for brothers in the early years because we both had moustaches and glasses. Davy is a wonderful guy who always sticks by his own ethics; a real family man and most of all, an amazing singer and brilliant drummer. I don't think I've ever played with a better drummer.

The second member of Clubsound I would like to thank is Barry Woods. Barry joined the band at a later stage and he has been a great friend. Barry and I have travelled together to all of the shows. He has made an amazing contribution to Clubsound over the years by simply being a brilliant musician. He plays many instruments, and, of course, he is a great vocaliser as well.

The next member of Clubsound that I would like to thank is Alan McCartney who joined the band at a later stage as well. Like Davy and Barry, Alan was brought up in the showband years when he played in different showbands. He is a brilliant guitarist and plays a variety of instruments, and is also renowned for his very deep voice. He is a talented composer and musical arranger, just like Barry.

Finally, the last member of Clubsound I would like to thank is, of course, Jimmy Black. Jimmy is a fine guitarist and great vocalist. Jimmy and I have travelled the world together too, not just with Clubsound, but he is also part of the band that went skiing for thirty years. Jimmy is a great family man and is always full of fun and laughter.

They are my four brothers, through the world of music not through family ties, and it has been a great honour to work with them under the name of Clubsound for the last fifty-plus years. These are three showbands that members of Clubsound have also played with — Barry Woods played with the Newmen showband, Alan McCartney with the Plattermen and Davy McKnight with the Freshmen. These were some of Northern Ireland's number one bands.

Now there is one person, who was an original member of Clubsound, and even though he didn't want to travel with the band, he will always remain close to my heart and deserves a special mention. When it comes to sharing thanks with people, I cannot emphasise enough the huge gratitude that I have for the late Tommy Thomas. What I discovered in Tommy was an absolute genius of the mind as well as being a genius as a musician. Without Tommy, Clubsound would never have existed and I want to pay a special tribute to him. He brought out the comedy in me, which I didn't realise I had, through his wonderful scriptwriting. At his funeral, I felt that I had lost a dear friend, a person who had inspired me so much, and I will constantly thank him for this until I leave this world.

Thanks, must also go to the late Jack Rogers, who I mentioned earlier in the book, who took Clubsound to America. He also took Clubsound to higher climes that we could never have imagined. It was through his ingenuity and his foresight that Clubsound became a household name in Northern Ireland; I miss him terribly. He was also a friend who was taken much too early in life, and I would love to be able to meet up with him and talk to him today.

I must also mention my dear friend David Hull. David has run a very successful promotions agency for many years.

He has been the agent for Clubsound and me for many years right up to present day. He has always stood by us over the years; he believed in me and the band and always would jokingly said, "I made my first £100 with Clubsound and lost my first £100 with them too."

When I came to him with the idea of the showband show, *Do You Come Here Often?*, he embraced it and took it on. Little did we know it would last for twenty-one years at the Waterfront Hall.

He also embraced my idea of *Rock 'n' Roll Years* and *Dance Hall Days Musical* which has been running successfully for the last seven years. I owe a lot to David and I would like to thank him for his trust and belief in me and the band.

Another on my list of thanks is an absolute gentleman — Joe Mullholland. You might remember me mentioning that he was the owner of the Railway Bar in Antrim. He also had great faith in Clubsound and allowed us to be the resident band in his bar for three and a half years. The happiness on his face that I used to see every time Clubsound played, said it all. We still meet up occasionally and he constantly thanks me and the guys in Clubsound for the wonderful years we shared with him and his father in their pub.

I would like to mention those who helped me get into radio and those who helped me through my radio career. Martin Dillion and Bob Crooks, gave me an opportunity to take over from Paul Clark. I had various producers, including the lovely Cherrie McIlwaine, who I have always considered to be one of the best voices on Radio Ulster. In addition, Pauline Curry, who enlisted me at the very beginning.

Janet Dougan, was one of my first personal assistants who helped me so much in those years. She was a wonderful, dedicated person, and then there was Gillian Kidd, when I became independent. Ian Kennedy and John Nicholson had great faith in me and inspired me to attain the most out of radio and then later on in television productions.

Most of all, I would like to thank a woman who has become a dear friend and had a wonderful input in helping me with my radio career; that is Liz Kennedy. I would like to take this opportunity to thank her for her wonderful help and encouragement. It was with her ingenious talent as a producer that I was privileged to interview so many famous people, not just in the studio, but around the world. I probably couldn't have achieved this without her.

Over the years I have been blessed with so many friends around the world and throughout my life. I am sure that there are many more stories that I could have added, but if I did, this would probably turn out to be the size of two volumes of yellow pages put together. But in just a few words, I wish to thank everyone for the friendship and help that I've received along life's journey.

As I finish this book I am currently in the middle of *Clubsound Farewell Theatre Tour.* We had an amazing fifty-two years. Never in our wildest expectations did we imagine we would last this long and become a household name. We feel very proud.

Clubsound on their farewell tour, 52 years later, 2022.

You're likely thinking, when is he going to hang up his boots? Let's give it a few more days or as I like now to put it … my days are in God's hands.

Right now, am playing bass in the *Elvis Spectacular Show* with some wonderful people keeping the king's music alive — Ciaran Houlighan as Elvis, and let me say … doing a brilliant job. Stevie Thompson and Gerry Rooney on keyboards. The Sweet Sensations who are, Kerry Smylie, Nadine Savage and Catherine McCallum. On guitar, *The Boss* Mervyn Boyd, who has kept the show together for twenty-five years. Then, of course, my good buddy in the engine room with me, an amazing powerhouse of a drummer — Graham Kincade.

Finally, something that is very close to my heart for the last year or so is helping to put together a wonderful new gospel band, which we have called Heart and Soul. Named after the inspirational television series I presented live from the Opera House some years ago.

These people are a wonderful bunch of Christians. I am so very fond of them all.

On keyboard the band features a wonderful talented player and singer Joy McIlwrath. One of the best I have heard for a long time. On guitar a super musician and guitarist from none other than Portstewart. Where is that? Only joking. Paul Wiseman a delight to play music with. On drums a super guy and great player Phillip Cairns. On trumpet and flugel horn — a dear friend who introduced me to the band, chief supreme — Stephen Jeffers.

The more I play with these wonderful people the more I'm inclined to believe that God is guiding me to play music in the future and I'm getting that message clearly every day. I'm really enjoying creating our particular treatment of great praise songs.

As I say goodbye at the end of my journey, I would like to think that people have shared this *helter-skelter* of a life with me, in the joyous and the depressing moments too, and that you will all find God, just as I have, but hopefully not as late as I did.

I hope that you have enjoyed sharing my journey in this book. If you like it, please keep it and feel free to share it. If you don't like it, well there's enough pages in it to use as firelighters for many years. So, for now, as I finish this book, goodbye to you all. I have to go — the show calls, or in truth God calls and I must go.

I'm still amazed at all what God has done.

PS. Sadie says goodbye to you as well.

CONTACT DETAILS

To invite George Jones to speak at your event, please email
events@MauriceWylieMedia.com

INSPIRED TO WRITE A BOOK?

Contact

Maurice Wylie Media

Your Inspirational & Christian Publisher

Based in Northern Ireland and distributing around the world.
www.MauriceWylieMedia.com